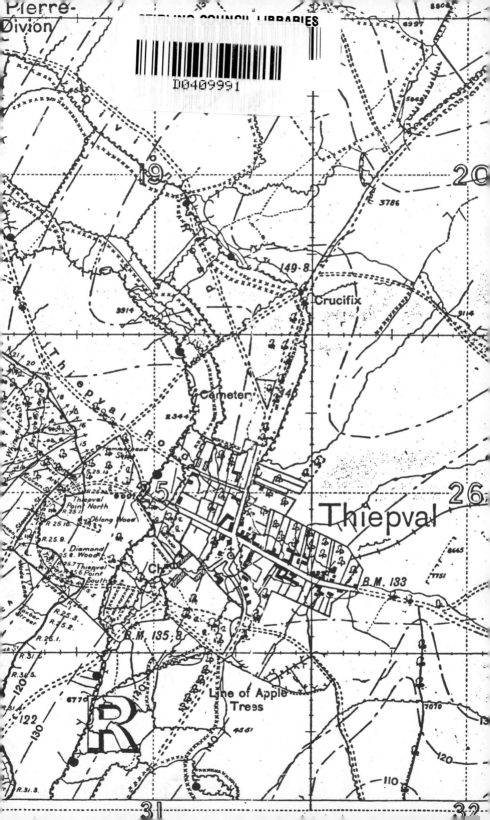

Pierre-
Divion

19

20

3786

149.8

Crucifix

3914

9114

Cemetery

140

2344

Thiepval Ro

Hamel head
Sap

15

R.25.13

5

26

Thiepval
Point North

Thiepval

R.25.11

Oblong Wood

R.25.10

R.25.9

Diamond
Wood

8665

R.25.8

7751

R.25.7 Thiepval
Point
South

Ch

B.M. 133

R.25.3

R.25.2

R.26.1

B.M. 135.8

R.31.6

R.31.5

120

R

Line of Apple
Trees

122

130

6776

7070

4561

120

110

R.31.8

31

32

Can't shoot a man
with a cold

Front endpaper:
Hammerhead Sap and Paisley Avenue, Thiepval (in German hands).

Endpapers – Courtesy: Imperial War Museum and Western Front Association

Orival Wood Cemetery with Mackintosh's grave

Can't shoot a man with a cold

Lt. E. Alan Mackintosh MC *1893–1917*
POET OF THE HIGHLAND DIVISION

COLIN CAMPBELL
ROSALIND GREEN

Argyll
publishing

© Colin Campbell & Rosalind Green 2004

First Published by
Argyll Publishing
Glendaruel
Argyll PA22 3AE
Scotland
www.argyllpublishing.com

British Library Cataloguing-in-Publication Data.
A catalogue record for this book is available from
the British Library.

ISBN 1 902831 76 4

Origination
        Cordfall Ltd, Glasgow
Printing & Binding
        St Edmundsbury Press Ltd, Bury St Edmunds, Suffolk

This book is dedicated to
Alan Mackintosh
and the friends for whom he returned to France.

IN NO MAN'S LAND

The hedge on the left, and the trench on the right,
And the whispering, rustling wood between,
And who knows where in the wood tonight,
Death or capture may lurk unseen,
The open field and the figures lying
Under the shade of the apple trees –
Is it the wind in the branches sighing
Or a German trying to stop a sneeze.

Louder the voices of night come thronging,
But over them all the sound is clear,
Taking me back to the place of my longing
And the cultured sneezes I used to hear,
Lecture-time and my tutor's 'hanker'
Stopping his period's rounded close,
Like the frozen hand of a German ranker
Down in a ditch with a cold in his nose.

I'm cold too, and a stealthy shuffle
From the man with a pistol covering me,
And the Bosche moving off with a snap and a shuffle
Break the windows of memory –
I can't make sure till the moon gets lighter –
Anyway, shooting is over bold,
Oh, damn you, get back to your trench, you blighter,
I really can't shoot a man with a cold.

Hammerhead Wood, Thiepval, 1915
A Highland Regiment

Contents

ACKNOWLEDGEMENTS

We are grateful for the assistance of the following people and organisations, who supplied us with vital information, directed us to better sources, or confirmed or indicated that we were exploring some blind alleys! We thank them all for their interest and support:

Maureen Addis, Lurgan Hospital, Co. Armagh; Robert Aldous, Society of Friends; Christine Allinson, Assistant Records Officer, The General Council of the Bar; Ruth Allinson, Jessop's Hospital, Sheffield; A.J.Baxendale, Official Receiver; Rosemary Beazley, niece of Alan Mackintosh; Michael Bott, Reading University Library; Simon Blundell, Librarian, The Reform Club, London; Colin Bruce, Department of Printed Books, Imperial War Museum; The Brighton Evening Argus; Ally Budge, Wick; Sue Cameron, The General Register Office for Scotland; The Chelmsford and South Woodham Weekly News; Colin Clarkson, Head of Reference Library, Cambridge University Library; The Commonwealth War Graves Commission, Enquiries Department; The County Archivist, Essex; L.T.Cramp, Official Receiver; Rosamund Cummings, Assistant Archivist, Library of the Religious Society of Friends, Friends' House, London; Dr. Mark Curthoys, Archivist, Christ Church, Oxford; Christopher Dean, Archivist, St.Paul's School, London; Geoffrey Dearmer; Rev. James Dewar; Julian Duffus, Research Historian and Genealogist; Tabitha Driver, Assistant Librarian, Friends' House, London; Rev. Dr. Susan Durber, Oxford; Janet Edgell, Librarian and Keeper of the Records, The Honourable Society of the Middle Temple, London; Charles Elliott; Lt.Col.Angus Fairrie (Rtd.), The Queen's Own Highlanders Regimental Museum; G.Fleet, Estates Bursar, St.John's College, Oxford; Ivy Forsyth and her niece Susan Slade; Kate Forteath, Oxford University Officers Training Corps; The General Register Office; Sue Goddard; Arthur Green, Downpatrick, Northern Ireland; Stephanie Green, Reference Team Librarian, Local Studies,

Brighton Area Libraries; Peter Harris, Hon.Archivist and Art Curator, The National Liberal Club, London; Mrs C. Holmes; Dick Holt,The Times library Archives, London; Linda A. Homfray, Assistant Archivist, Christ Church, Oxford; Dr.W.P.Honeyman; Heather M. Hornbrook; Kevin Jones, Norfolk; Martin Jones, Hon. Archivist, Brighton College, Sussex; J.E.Kelly, Head of CS(RM)2, Ministry of Defence (Records); Kilbarchan Community Library, Renfrewshire; Killamarsh Library, Derbyshire; Raymonde and Claude Lesniak, Cantaing; Alice Lock, Local Studies Librarian, Tameside Local Studies Library, Astley Cheetham Public Libray, Stalybridge; James Loughran, The Somme Association, Belfast; Catherine Mackay, Park School, Invergordon; A.Mackintosh, Worthing, West Sussex; A.I.D.Mackintosh, Worthing; A.J.Mackintosh, Solicitor, Birmingham; D.A.Mackintosh, Eastbourne; Duncan R. Mackintosh, Eastbourne; J.D.M.Mackintosh, Solicitor, Surrey; John MacLennan, Black Isle; Alistair Macleod, Genealogist, Highland Regional Council; Margaret MacQuarrie; Major A.J.Maher (Rtd.), The Queen's Lancashire Regiment, Preston; Veronica Marchbanks, Archives Assistant, British Red Cross; The Mitchell Library, Glasgow; Rev John Miller, Rhonehouse; T.Mitra, General Medical Council; Roderick Morrison, Port of Ness; S. Ann Morton, Society of Friends, Ulster; Willie Morrison, The Press and Journal, Dingwall; Ian Mouland, Personnel, The Insolvency Services; Andrew Neil, Editor, The Sunday Times; The New Zealand High Commission; Susan E. Odell, Academic Division, University of Exeter; Doraine Patience, Researcher, Alness; Michael Petty, Principal librarian, Local Studies, Cambridgeshire; Ann Powell, The Western Front Association; The Probate Registry, York; The Search Department, Public Record Office, London; Dr.Marjorie Reeves, Oxford;Captain J.A.Roberts R.E., Cambridge University Officers Training Corps; Irene Rowan, Librarian; M.M.Rowe, County Archivist, Devon; Philip Rundle, Hon.Archivist, Cambridge University Teaching Hospitals Trust; Robert Satchwell, Editor, Cambridge Evening News; Robert Steward, Regional Archivist, Highland Regional Council, Inverness; William Stingone, for the Research Librarian, The Harry Ransom Humanities Research Center, University of Texas at Austin; Mike A. Stollery, Hove, Sussex; Richard Storey, Archivist, Modern Records Centre, University Library, University of Warwick; Hew Strachan, Professor of History,

Glasgow; David Sutherland, Caithness; Iain Sutherland, Wick Heritage Centre; W.F.Swarbrick, The Congregational Centre, Nottingham; Martin Taylor, Department of Printed Books, Imperial War Museum; Shaun Thomas, Earls Colne; L.C.Topliffe, Sub-librarian, Exeter College, Oxford; Steven Tomlinson, The Department of Western Manuscripts, The Bodleian Library, Oxford; Ian Trushell, Kilbarchan; Dr.Malcolm Vale, Keeper of the Archives, St.John's College, Oxford; Tara Wenger, Harry Ransom Humanities Research Centre; Stephen White, Local History Librarian, Carlisle Library; Waterthorpe and Central Libraries, Sheffield City Libraries; Stephen White, Local History Librarian, Carlisle Library; Charlotte Zeepvat, Researcher;

Thanks also to K.O.Y.L.I Battlefield Pilgrimages and the War Research Society for friendship and assistance during Western Front tours.

And to Evelyn Campbell and Trevor Green, who have supported and encouraged the authors during this project.

We are indebted to the following who have given us permission to reprint from copyright material:

Rosemary Beazley and Elizabeth Eden, for extracts from *A Highland Regiment*, and *War, The Liberator* by E.A.Mackintosh, and Alan and Lillian Mackintosh's letters and photographs; Harry Ransom Humanities Research Centre, University of Texas at Austin, for extracts from letters by E.A.Mackintosh and Lilian Mackintosh; Mrs Pamela MacLennan, Culbokie, Black Isle, for material supplied by the late John MacLennan; Carcanet Press Limited, for permission to reproduce extracts from *Goodbye to All That* by Robert Graves (Jonathan Cape, 1929); Hodder & Stoughton Limited for permission to reproduce extracts from *The Fifty-First in France* by Captain Robert B. Ross; George Alpine, for extracts from *A Medico's Luck in the War* by David Rorie (Milne and Hutchison).

Efforts have been made to contact other copyright holders, or their descendants, literary executors or publishers, and we apologise for any omissions. Acknowledgement will be made in future editions if the appropriate information is made available to us.

E. Alan Mackintosh.

Ewart Alan Mackintosh,
Second Lieutenant, Seaforth Highlanders,
1/5th (Sutherland and Caithness) Battalion
Gazetted 1st January 1915

PROLOGUE

Ewart Alan Mackintosh aspired to be a poet. He wrote poetry in school, university and the army, and before he went to the Western Front for the first time arranged in his will for an anthology to be published. Although his poems are uneven in quality, and reflect highs and lows of his experience, he worked at his writing, and wanted to be judged as a poet. But he was also a schoolboy, a student, a man in love, and a soldier.

This book has been written to explore these many facets of Mackintosh's short life. Being a poet numbers him amongst a tiny minority: as a soldier he shared his experience with millions. His life must therefore be reflected against the background of the most brutal and expensive war then known to history.

The First World War was the outcome of a fatal concoction of aggressive nationalism, prejudice, blind patriotism, and economic competition. It was initially sustained by the peoples of Europe who had been conditioned to accept and respect their governments. Both sides were innocently optimistic about the likely length of the war, and thought that it would be 'over by Christmas'. By November 1914 the war of manoeuvre was over and the static trench warfare that characterised the Western Front was well established. The armies faced each other from lines of ditches, hacked out of chalk or clay. Where the water table was too close to the surface breastworks of sandbags were built. Each trench system was protected by barbed wire entanglements. Behind the front line trenches were support and reserve trenches, connected to one another and the relative safety of the rear, by communication trenches.

No Man's Land lay between the opposing wire entanglements: it could extend for a mile, or be as little as a few yards, and was littered with human remains and the material debris of battle, broken by shell holes, and infested with corpse rats. Most casualties were caused by shelling, which crashed on the trenches, demolishing them, wounding or fragmenting their occupants, or burying them as the sides caved in. Snipers shot the careless, the indifferent, the unlucky and the suicidal. Where the geology was appropriate mines were tunneled beneath enemy trenches, explosives detonated and the crater occupied by attacking infantry.

Attacks were preceded by artillery bombardments on the enemy trenches and supply routes. Early in the war these did little damage as the British were short of shells, but by 1916 they were so destructive that advancing infantry often found the battlefield almost impassable. The conclusion of the barrage, or its forward movement, alerted the enemy to the inevitable infantry attack. Led by their junior officers the soldiers clambered out of their trenches to be met by the withering rifle and machine gun fire of the enemy who had survived the shelling. Units that did reach the enemy's front line were almost invariably trapped there or forced to withdraw, as the enemy's artillery cut them off from supplies and reinforcements.

It was a measure of the patriotism, mutual loyalty and obedience of the men that battalions that had been reduced in battle by half or more, would, after a short rest and reinforcements, go back to give and take more punishment. Although there were firing squads for deserters, it is an insulting over-simplification to suggest that this was the sole motive for going forward.

A battalion at full strength numbered 1,000 men. During the war the battalion featured in this book, the 1/5th Seaforth Highlanders, had 5522 men of all ranks pass through it. Of these 730 were killed, 2485 wounded and 300 were pronounced missing, presumed dead.[1] These statistics are typical of many infantry battalions in France. By 1919, 3.1% of Scotland's adult male population had been killed, against 1.6% of the male population of the British Isles. This was partly attributable to Scotland having a disproportionately large number of regular and territorial infantry regiments, all of which recruited new battalions, and partly to Scottish units being successful in assault, and being regularly deployed as shock troops, with concomitant high casualties.

While the principle reason for deadlock was the ability of sufficient defenders to survive a bombardment and emerge with their weapons intact, a number of other factors contributed to the failure of the British. Neuve Chapelle in May 1915 failed through

---

(1) Page 3, War Diary of the 5th Seaforth Highlanders, Captain
   D. Sutherland. John Lane, 1920.

lack of artillery preparation. Loos, in September 1915, saw the advantages of a two mile penetration through the German lines by the 15th Scottish Division lost by the surviving troops going astray due to inexperienced leadership and the fog of war, by tired raw reserves being thrown into battle, and by the best reserves being retained too far from the front – a combination of bad leadership, poor planning and inadequate training.

The 20,000 dead and 38,000 wounded on the first day of the Battle of the Somme, 1st July 1916, can be attributed to over-optimism by the generals, bad intelligence, and the failure of the artillery to destroy the enemy wire and the deeply dug-in German defenders. The advances on the Somme from July until November 1916 cost 420,000 British casualties, and took the British between two and eight miles from their start line. The Third Battle of Ypres (Passchedaele) in August 1917 took place in Flemish weather conditions which should have ensured a postponement; in mud which made the use of tanks an absurdity, and the deployment of troops a crime.

Until the autumn of 1917 the war was of a series of hopes dashed, lives expended, enthusiasm exhausted, and hard lessons learned, for gains that were measured in yards. The first day of the Battle of Cambrai, on 20th November 1917, punched a hole in the German front line, and seemed to herald an end to trenchlock on the Western Front. In Spring 1917 the Germans had retired to the newly constructed Hindenberg Line. This well-sited triple trench system was over four miles deep in places, with fifty metres width of barbed wire in front of each line of trenches. Some trenches were broad enough to ditch tanks, and innumerable concrete machine gun positions had been built.

The key element by the British was the surprise use of massed tanks, which had rehearsed trench clearing tactics with their supporting infantry. Tanks were detailed to roll up the barbed wire with grapnels. The tanks had been moved into position behind the British lines under cover of darkness, and of the noise of artillery and aircraft. To avoid warning the enemy or making the ground impassable to tanks, the thousand gun barrage began as the three hundred and fifty tanks moved forward, disguising the noise of their movement and keeping the enemy's heads down. To cross wide trenches the tanks carried huge bundles of brushwood, which they dropped into them, and then drove over.

The tanks and infantry rapidly carved their way through impotent and initially demoralised German defences. There was a hold-up with the 51st (Highland) Division, arguably because its General Harper had ignored the tactics laid down for infantry and tank co-operation, and kept his infantry too far behind the tanks. In addition a German artilleryman at Flesquières Ridge destroyed five tanks, and slowed the advance.

Later on the 21st tanks scheduled to co-operate with the Highland Division's advance were delayed and its 154th Brigade went into action without them. The 4th Gordon Highlanders and the 7th Argyll and Sutherland Highlanders led the attack, followed by the 9th Royal Scots and the 4th Seaforth Highlanders.[2]

In No.4 Company of the 4th Seaforth Highlanders a tall, lean, bespectacled lieutenant, with very bad eyesight, and a limp, advanced with his platoon. He wore the purple and white ribbon of the Military Cross, and a Sutherland tartan kilt, unlike the Mackenzie worn by his men. He was Lieutenant E. Alan Mackintosh MC, 5th Seaforth Highlanders, who had been attached to the 4th Seaforth Highlanders for six weeks.[3]

He was then twenty four years old and had recently become engaged to a girl with whom he hoped to emigrate to New Zealand after the war. Alan Mackintosh was no gullible innocent, taking part in his first campaign. He had a year's front line service, an award for gallantry, and had been wounded and gassed. After his convalescence he had an important job training officer cadets in Cambridge. Modern assessments of his situation before returning to France in 1917 would suggest that he had made a substantial personal contribution to the war effort, and that he could have spent the rest of the war in Britain with a clear conscience: his engagement in 1917 adds force to this. However, he volunteered to go back to France, a conscious decision made by many others who could have stayed at home.

Much of what Alan Mackintosh said, thought and did, as a young man and an officer may now seem mildly absurd. That is only

---

(2) Page 250, The History of the 51st Highland Division 1914-
    1918, F.W. Bewsher. Blackwood, 1921.

(3) 4th Seaforths' war diary, Queen's Own Highlanders museum,
    Fort George, Inverness.

justifiable if we ignore his background; or if hindsight is a legitimate basis for judgment. It is not. Our hindsight was bought at the expense of Mackintosh and his generation, and the succeeding generation, and their sacrifice has coloured our approach to patriotism, war, and the international community.

Young 5th Seaforths from Achreamie/Buldoo (population *circa* 60) Caithness
left to right:
Sandy Henderson (killed); William Henderson (brother of Sandy);
James Baikie (killed); unknown; David Sutherland (killed); unknown

INTRODUCTION

In the pre-1914 decade people conducted themselves within parameters that now seem extremely limiting. A largely unenfranchised and minimally educated working population existed, used to low wages, bad living conditions and varying degrees of social and commercial servility.

Those who cared to think about it realised that they were part of the greatest empire in the world, and that they could emigrate if they needed to leave home. Although imperialism and exploitation now seem synonymous, it was believed that 'uncivilised' peoples benefited from British colonial domination. Many regarded taking up the 'white man's burden' in Africa and India as a Christian duty. 'My country right or wrong' best expresses the type of unquestioning patriotism that existed before 1914. Devoid of our twenty-first century instant exposure to lives and events throughout the world, it was simple for governments and a patriotic press to convince the general population of threats, real or imagined, from abroad, and to perpetuate the idea that their nation was superior to, or should be superior to, all the other nations of the world. The Royal Navy's ability to outgun any fleet in the world, and to sail its seas with impunity was the early twentieth century equivalent of nuclear superiority. Empire Day was celebrated, with parades, special services, and flag waving: and everyone in the United Kingdom knew that it was an empire upon which the sun never set.

The notion of duty permeated every stratum of society and was particularly marked in Mackintosh's middle class and in the upper classes, and endured well into the war. A verse from a monthly magazine, the *Boy's Own Paper*, is typical:

Always be true to the skipper, my lad,
Always be trusty and true:
Mutinous spirit is worthless and bad,
Bad both for him and for you.

One must be leader, whatever the sport,
One must be chief in the fight;
Give to the captain your eager support –
Serve him in all that is right.[1]

All classes knew their place in a hierarchy that still often laid more stress on birth and connections than on individual merit. The Church, established or non-conformist, moulded an obedient population, and made its acceptance of the unpleasantness of life the price of happiness in the promised hereafter. While it is impossible to estimate how many people believed in immortality, it is certain that a far higher proportion than now were convinced that immortality was assured.

This enabled soldiers and civilians to tolerate the increasing burden of deaths in battle.

Out here you must trust yourself to a bigger Power and leave it at that. You can't face death. There's no facing it. It's everywhere. You have to walk through it, and under it, and over it and past it. Without the sense of God taking up the souls of those poor torn bodies – even though they have died cursing Him – I think one would go mad.[2]

Society was hard: education was characterised by rote learning and corporal punishment; prisons were for punishment, not rehabilitation; juvenile offenders were often birched, and capital punishment was normal for murderers. Homosexuality was illegal, the children of unmarried mothers were often scorned as bastards or consigned to children's homes, divorce was rare, and the husband was the head of the home.

Entertainment took place in concert halls and theatres, and a few cinemas showed flickering black and white silent films. Wireless telegraphy was in its infancy, and newspapers the source of most information. International travel was by ship or train, and regular services by both linked the UK to the rest of the world. Medical

---

(1) Page 460 Boy's Own Paper 20th April 1912

(2) Captain T.P.C. Wilson, 10th Sherwood Foresters in *War Letters of Fallen Englishmen* (ed. Laurence Housman), page 296. Gollancz, 1930

science was advancing, but tuberculosis was usually fatal, appendectomies had just been mastered, infected wounds developed gas gangrene, and dentistry was often carried out without anaesthetics.

The armed forces were a bastion of privilege, with peacetime officers drawn from the real or would-be aristocracy. The infusion of temporary officers during the war troubled some of them deeply. Their snobbery extended to making distinctions between Regular, Kitchener's New Army, and Territorial battalions. Regular officers had often regarded the Territorial Forces with scorn, and the fact that Kitchener's Army was a regular force did not prevent them mocking the influx of inexperienced amateur enthusiasts who had only signed on 'for the duration' of the war.

The pejorative 'temporary gentlemen' was applied to the newcomers, and at the start of the war some Regulars went out of their way to make them unwelcome. In some officers' messes new 'duration only' officers were shunned by unenlightened professionals. Robert Graves in *Goodbye to All That* was told on his arrival in France at his regular Royal Welch Fusiliers battalion:

> The senior officers are beasts. If you open your mouth
> or make the slightest sound, they jump down your
> throat. Only officers of the rank of captain are allowed
> to drink whisky or turn on the gramophone.[3]

By the end of the war, the newcomers were in the majority.

Discipline for the men was strict, and field punishment Number One entailed the soldier being tied to a cartwheel or to a specially constructed T-shaped post, for a number of hours, in view of his colleagues. Post-traumatic stress was unknown by that name. Shell shock was recognised by the front line troops, and they did not condemn those who suffered it: to most civilians and staff officers it was a euphemism for cowardice.

By 1917 the well of unthinking patriotism which had fuelled the early stages of the war still existed, even amongst a population increasingly numbed by casualties. Although patriotism became a joke with many soldiers, it had been replaced by a ferocious loyalty to one's comrades, and, by extension of that, to one's battalion.

---

(3) Page 106 Goodbye to All That Robert Graves. Jonathan Cape
    1929

This loyalty was so well developed that, for most, the only acceptable escape from the front was by attaining a 'Blighty' (Hindustani for 'home') wound, one severe enough to make return to the UK inevitable and preferably irreversible. Anything more would kill or maim unpleasantly, and anything less would mean recuperation and return to the front.

The horror of their shared experience bound them as nothing else could, and isolated them from a civilian population which was protected from the realities by a press that was underinformed or misinformed by the General Staff.

The soldiers belittled the conditions at the front:'He does nothing by his speech to help people at home to realise the hell he has lived through,' wrote Coningsby Dawson of soldiers on leave.[4]

This was the social and military world that Mackintosh inhabited. Whether he was a minor poet or an as yet unrecognised major poet is not for the authors to decide. If, as William Owen said, 'The poetry is in the pity' and if Owen's poems are heralded for their revelation of that pity, then Mackintosh merits more recognition than he has had to date.

---

(4) *War, The Liberator*, E.A.Mackintosh. John Lane,The Bodley Head, 1918. (Introduction by Coningsby Dawson in later edition)

RETURN

Oh! I have loved the city
(It was long ago)
And stretched my arms towards her,
Her beauty and her woe;
But now I turn me back again
To the country that I know.

For us that loved the city
Our love has passed away,
And we are left all loveless
And naked to the day;
And so we all creep home again
Upon the Downs to play.

The gentle swelling Downland
Stands clear against the sky,
There, where a man must struggle back,
Upon her breast to lie,
And think he is a little child
While all his life slips by.

So when our hearts are bitter,
And smirched with blot and stain,
And fruit has turned to ashes,
And all our joy is pain,
Thank God upon the Downland
We're children once again.

'The Pauline'

TO CATULLUS
A Rondel

Laughter and tears to you the gods once gave,
Those silver tears upon your brother's grave,
And golden laughter in your lady's bower,
And silver-gold in your love's bitter hour.
You showed us, burdened with our hopes and fears,
    Laughter and tears.

Poor tears that fell upon the thirsty sands,
Poor laughter stifled with ungentle hands,
Poor heart that was so sweet to laugh and cry,
Your joyful, mournful songs shall never die,
But show us still across the shadowing years
    Laughter and tears.

St. Paul's 1912
A Highland Regiment

MALLAIG BAY

I am sickened by the south and the kingdom of the downs,
    And the weald that is a garden all the day.
And I'm weary for the islands and the Scuir that always frowns,
    And the sun rising over Mallaig Bay.

I am sickened of the pleasant down and pleasant weald below,
    And the meadows where the little breezes play,
And I'm weary for the rain-cloud over stormy Coolin's brow,
    And the wind blowing into Mallaig Bay.

I am sickened of the people that have ease in what they earn,
    The happy folk who have forgot to pray,
And I'm weary for the faces that are sorrowful and stern,
    And the boats coming into Mallaig Bay.

Sussex, 1912
A Highland Regiment

TO THE UNKNOWN LOVE

I cannot see you in the light
Or find you in the day,
For when the sun springs up at dawn
I think you slip away.

I wait until the night is come
To pass beyond the veil,
And then I find you in the land
Of the unuttered tale.

Then gazing out across the night
I see with wild surmise
The shadows of your loosened hair,
The depth of your grave eyes.

St.Paul's 1912
A Highland Regiment

CHAPTER I

CHILDHOOD AND YOUTH

But now I turn me back again
To the country that I know.

'Return', The Pauline

Mackintosh's paternal family was Scottish. His grandparents were Angus and Janet Mackintosh and the parochial register of Daviot and Dunlichty, near Inverness[1] records the baptism of their son Alexander on 5th October 1837. They farmed at Beachan, Farr, near Inverness. Alexander Mackintosh married Janet Cameron and after her death he married his second wife Lilian on 25th June 1879 at the Clapham Congregational Church. Lilian was twenty years old, and the wedding certificate describes Alexander as being 'of full age'! He was then forty-two, twenty-two years her senior.

During his first marriage Alexander had travelled to India, and birth places in the 1881 census show that he had travelled and lived in England in the course of his business. The Ross-shire valuation rolls from 1868 to 1881, and the 1881 census, show that Alexander occupied Teaninich House, near Alness. Teaninich is a substantial residence standing on land which had belonged to the Munro family from the seventeenth century. Alexander rented it from its owner, Stewart Caradoc Munro.[2]

Lilian was the daughter of Dr. Guinness Rodgers, a famous non-conformist preacher, who was very friendly with the Liberal leader, William Ewart Gladstone. When Dr. Rodgers visited him at his house at Hawarden he recorded: 'the kindness and attention of Mr. Gladstone were past description. He took me over the grounds and showed me some of his favourite spots.'

---

(1) General Register Office for Scotland, Edinburgh
(2) Doraine Patience

When the time came to leave, Gladstone: 'insisted on escorting me to the station. It happened that I had to cross the line for the train and my great anxiety was to keep him from accompanying me. But remonstrance was all in vain. The courtesy of the true gentleman seemed to banish every other consideration from him.'[3] They were such close friends that during the 1892 election campaign Gladstone spoke at a meeting in the Rodgers' house in Clapham.

Between 1882, when a daughter Lilian Violet was born, and 1888, when Muriel was born, the Mackintosh family had made its home in Brighton. The 1891 census includes two of Lilian Violet and Muriel's three older sisters and their older brother Aeneas. A second son, Alick, born between the births of Lilian Violet and Muriel, died at the age of two.[4]

The family had a succession of Brighton addresses: in 1885 they were living at 39 Bond Street; by 1891, 3 Clarendon Terrace: and finally, in 1905, 6 Sussex Square. Alexander's office was at 4 Pavilion Buildings.[5]

Aeneas, the only son of his first marriage, was called to the Bar on 15th May 1889, practised on the South East circuit, and was involved with the Sussex, North London and Middlesex Sessions from about 1895 to 1906. He occupied chambers at 1 Brick Court from 1891 to 1894.[6] His name is not in the Law Lists after 1906 and in Murray's Memoir Alan is referred to as the only survivingson of Alexander Mackintosh. It is known that Aeneas died in Canada.[7]

Alan Mackintosh was the only surviving son of Alexander's second marriage, and the youngest of the family. He was born on 4th March 1893, at 3 Clarendon Terrace, Brighton. His full name was Ewart Alan Mackintosh. The Ewart forename was a tribute to his mother's family's happy association with Gladstone. The fact that he did not use it when he grew up may indicate that he did not

(3) Page 233 *An Autobiography* J. Guinness Rodgers. Clarke and Co., London, 1903

(4) Family evidence, Rosemary Beazley (daughter of Muriel Mackintosh)

(5) Brighton street directories, 1885, 1889 and 1901, per Stephanie Green, Brighton Area Libraries

(6) Honourable Society of the Middle Temple. M. Jones

(7) Family evidence, Rosemary Beazley (daughter of Muriel Mackintosh)

like it, although there was a fashion then for preceding the customary name with the initial of the first name.

Although he was the youngest child, he was strictly raised. He was educated at home with his sisters and thus his formative years were within the confines of the family, characterised by the chasm of formality that separated parents from children, with nannies and governesses being totally responsible for the practicalities of child raising. A routine of nursery, home classroom, and supervised outings would have made spontaneous friendships with a cross-section of children an unfamiliar experience.

In January 1905, at the age of twelve, he was admitted to the Junior House of Brighton College. There he would have widened his circle of friends, and developed social skills in group situations. He remained there as a day boy until July 1909 and won the IVth Form English Prize in 1907, and the VIth Form Greek History Prize in 1908. In his last session he was in the debating society.

Mackintosh's name does not appear in any team lists at Brighton College.[8] His lack of athleticism may have been attributable to childhood illness. John Murray says in his 'Memoir' of him as a soldier: 'with growing strength and health he grew in the control of his own powers and in influence over other men.' That this was noteworthy suggests that he had not enjoyed normal health in his childhood and adolescence. In a schoolboy society that valued physical prowess and put a premium on team games, and which often stigmatised the intellectuals and the non-athletes, Mackintosh may have had some difficulty in integrating.

He won a scholarship to St.Paul's, then in Kensington, and went into the Middle VIIIth in 1909.[9] There is no record at St. Paul's of his showing any sporting prowess, but he participated regularly in the debating society.[10] Limited significance can be read into school debate minutes, as participants often have to argue for or against motions with little respect for their own points of view: this would be especially true in a society that gathered just over a dozen boys at its meetings. However, a few features emerge which carry over into his adulthood.

---

(8) Brighton College archives

(9) St. Paul's School archives

(10) St. Paul's debating society minutes, 1910-1912

There is evidence of his sense of humour: on February 10th 1910 'Mr. Mackintosh cracked a few quips' which were unmemorable enough not to be minuted. In a March 1911 debate on the lack of proper safety precautions against railway accidents he displayed a gruesome sense of humour in that he 'dealt with the matter from two points of view, the aesthetic and the ethical. He dilated on the aesthetic beauties of telescoped carriages in a railway accident. The great ethical point on which he laid stress was the uncertainty of our destination – it might be Brighton or Hades.'

He had an adolescent's inclination to attack sacred cows: in October 1911, speaking on the rights and wrongs of the Home Office in stopping a boxing match he said, 'What was the true art of England and the World? Music? Sculpture? Painting? No. Boxing. At this point Mr. Mackintosh sat down abruptly.' This suggests insufficient preparation, indications of which are to be found in his school reports. In a motion on the 7th of April 1910 that 'This House considers the neglect of Browning and his contemporaries was unjustifiable' Alan Mackintosh seconded saying 'that any cultured nation was justified in neglecting such barbarous and unoriginal poetry as Browning's. There was nothing in Browning, or indeed, in any poet. He asked the House to vote against the motion because all poets were bad.' This is perhaps self-deprecatory, and he was possibly trying to eschew his poetic instincts, or perhaps he was simply trying to be iconoclastic.

His view on poets contrasts with his view of musical comedy: on 14th November 1910 he opposed the proposition that 'musical comedy is injurious to the interests of the stage', confessing that he 'liked the humour of comedies and the type of person to be found in the galleries.'

Imperialism was the norm and like most of his generation he supported it: on 21st November 1910 he opposed a call to the British government to 'restore to the Indians their liberty' saying 'We should keep the Indies for their own good.' Given his father Alexander's previous occupation as an East India merchant this was an unsurprising stance. Debating the then current and highly controversial topic of Irish Home Rule in March 1912 Alan stated that 'devolution was a good and patriotic thing', but made it clear that he was not in favour of Home Rule or total independence.

At the Fifty Eighth Anniversary Meeting of the society, in

September 1911, the movers of the motion 'disapproved of the Empire.' Mackintosh asserted that he was 'a devotee of (the) Imperialism.' The minute then states that he 'misquoted the other speakers and sat down.'

His family connections with Gladstone may have coloured his opinion of the Conservative Party. On February 2nd 1911 he was 'confident in the Liberal Government. There was no need of a conscript army, for, if ever our navy was destroyed by Germany, no British Army could save us. Let the cultured minds of the House beware the shameless fabrications of the Conservative Party.' The choice of this debate reflected the perceived German threat, and the attempts by Lord Roberts to persuade the government to begin conscription, and the common view that Britain could not match the size of the Continental armies.

On November 6th 1911 he referred to the 'awful degradation' of the Conservative Party. He seconded a motion disapproving of the public school system, in February 1912, an early indicator of his later flirtation with socialism.

Was he a racist? A debate welcoming 'more drastic restrictions on alien immigration' was proposed by Mackintosh, standing in for a Mr. Sainsbury. There are signs in the content of his speech that he enjoyed teasing people. The anarchist Peter the Painter had recently been shot in the siege of Sidney Street. Mackintosh said that 'in city states aliens had never been tolerated; that whereas such a type of alien as Peter the Painter soon died out, other foreigners were more subtle, insidious and viperous. We need such offspring of the British Lion as Mr. Horatio Bottomley to repel them from our shores.' (As a result of his second bankruptcy, Horatio Bottomley had resigned as MP for South Hackney: he owned various publications, including *John Bull*, which was a populist patriotic magazine).

He was opposed by Victor Gollancz who said, 'The day the Alien Bill was passed was a bad day for England, which up till then had been a land of freedom. There was no narrow patriotism in humanity.' As the debate continued Edmund Solomon and Victor Gollancz staged 'a dramatic exit', 'but both were prevailed upon to return.'

In his concluding speech Gollancz 'pointed out the world wide influence of Tchaikowsky, Goethe, Schiller (phonetic spelling!) and other foreigners. Beauty was conceived differently by different critics. The generally accepted stamp of a foreigner 'fat podginess and trumpet noses' might be lovely and attractive in the eyes of some. Mr. Mackintosh (in his concluding speech) declared his view of Art differed from those of the hon. opposer.'

Edmund Solomon and Victor Gollancz were Jewish. As Edmund Solomon became one of Mackintosh's closest friends in university, and was named as a beneficiary of Mackintosh's will, it suggests that Mackintosh was playing the devil's advocate in this debate.

Those who broke the society's code were disciplined. On 27th November 1912 the case was discussed of a member who 'had thrown a brush at a member while the latter was eating his lunch, and on being requested by an official not to repeat the offence, threw another brush, only just missing the member's front teeth.'

The member refused to apologise on the grounds that 'certain facial grimaces were distasteful to him. If the house elected disgusting members that was their look out.' Mackintosh's contribution to this storm over a school lunch and boyish clash of maturing personalities was to say that he had 'rarely heard a more disgusting exhibition. The attack on the House and one of its members was impertinent and in the worst possible taste.'

The episode seems trivial and Mackintosh's reaction prim: but before the First World War made breaking the rules acceptable to most of its participants, playing the game by the book was a well established and unalterable principle.

Mackintosh's school reports are revealing both of the boy and the staff:[11]

> July 1910 17 yrs 4 months, (at the end of his first
> session).Latin – capable boy: has (illegible) of
> accumulating knowledge. Thorough prig.

The Classic's teacher's judgment of him as a prig echoes his reaction to the schoolboy dispute over the thrown brushes.

> July 1911 18 yrs 4 months.
> Latin – has made reasonably good progress in Latin.

---

(11) St. Paul's School archives

Greek – improvement very slow but he tries hard. His
writing is a disgrace.
Divinity and English – one of the best essay writers in
the form: has greatly improved.
General: his English is rather good: his handwriting is
very bad.

The curriculum for the seventeen boys in the Upper VIIIth,
from January to July 1912, shows how much education has changed:

Divinity: The First Epistle to the Corinthians.
Latin: Cicero, Pro Plancio; Tacitus, Annals Bk.I; Virgil,
Aeneid, I – III; Verse and Prose Repetition: Virgil,
Aeneid IV, 1 – 362; Euripedes, Hecuba (Selections);
Golden Treasury (Selections).
History: English History, 1689 to the present day;
Greek History, The Pelopennesian War.
French: Erckmann – Chatrian, Waterloo; Victor Hugo,
Hernani; Cassel and Karcher's Senior Course of
Composition; Etymology; Dictation; Conversation;
Examination Papers.

July 1912 19 years 4 months.
Latin – needs continual keeping up to his work.
Greek – competent but has twice done excellent pieces
of work.
Divinity and English – V.good indeed.
General remarks – a very able boy but his masters are
agreed that he is not a pleasant pupil (in ink, and
deleted). He has plenty of ability but is not an easy pupil
to teach (in pencil, in the same hand).

The initial damning of his character may have been altered
soon after the ink report was written, after mature reflection; or it
could have been changed by the writer after Mackintosh's Military
Cross, his wound, his two anthologies, and death on the battlefield.

An overview of the reports suggests that Mackintosh was good
at what came easily to him, English and essay writing, and adequate
in subjects in which sustained effort was necessary. Some teachers

will recognise the pupil who is cleverer than most, and arrogant as a result, or the pupil who irritates the teacher by not fulfilling his potential in a subject, or appears not to be interested in it. Any combination of these, or simply a personality clash between the classics department and Alan Mackintosh could have led to the last unforgiving report.

Despite the restrained reports on his ability in classics, Mackintosh won a classical scholarship to Christ Church, Oxford, indicating that the high standards demanded by St. Paul's were in keeping with the requirements of Oxford: perhaps Mackintosh's classics teacher motivated his pupils by being scant with praise.

As editor of 'The Pauline', the school magazine, Mackintosh toyed with military metaphors in a report on the cutting back of Virginia creeper on the school building. 'It had delivered a sort of skirmishing attack on figure iv of the clock, and if it had been allowed to develop the assault it would have to have made a total capture of that important position. So it had to be suppressed – (translated to Latin) sufflaminandus erat; and we suppose the only really effective plan was the one adopted, viz. leaving a good wide buffer state between the enemy and the venerable gutters.'[12]

Three poems of Mackintosh's appear in 'The Pauline'. One is a rondel, 'To Catullus'[13] stemming from the classical bias of his education. He chose to include it in *A Highland Regiment*.

> You showed us, burdened with our hopes and fears,
> Laughter and tears.

The others relate to the Sussex Downs. The first verse of 'The Kingdom of the Downs',[14] is romantic, idealistic and contrived, but displays a genuine affection for his native Downs, It was written on the train between London and Brighton in 1911.

> Beyond the woodlands shading.
> Beyond the sun-kissed field,
> Where laughs in joy unfading

---

(12) 'The Pauline', St. Paul's archives

(13) 'The Pauline', St. Paul's archives, and page 58 *A Highland Regiment*

(14) Page 55, *A Highland Regiment*, E. A. Mackintosh

The garden of the Weald,
Look southward, where uplifted
Against the shining skies,
In secret vesture shifted,
The silent Downs arise.

'Return'[15] did not appear in his later anthologies but it introduces the recall of his childhood which features in later poems, including his war poems, as well as reinforcing his love of Sussex:

Thank God upon the Downland,
We're children once again.

'Mallaig Bay',[16] written in Sussex in 1912 is the antithesis of his eulogies of the Downs. Mallaig was and is a fishing port at the end of the West Highland line. Its prosperity had been built on the hard graft of fisher folk. The poem reveals disaffection with the south and a yearning for Scotland.

I am sickened of the south and the kindness of the downs
    And the weald that is a garden all the day,
And I'm weary for the islands and the Scuir that always frowns,
    And the sun rising over Mallaig Bay.

He travelled to Scotland before the war, not just to meet relations or because it was fashionable, but to absorb the language and culture of his forefathers. Were his reflections on the hardships faced by the West Coast fishermen merely a reaction against the lives led by office workers and professionals in the South, or a reflection of the conflict between his Highland ancestry and his English upbringing? There was another reason for his disillusionment with Brighton. He could not publish his most personal poem of this time in 'The Pauline', 'To the Unknown Love', for to have done so would have been to expose himself to the mockery and ribaldry of his peer group: he included it in *A Highland Regiment*:[17]

(15) 'The Pauline', St. Paul's archives

(16) *A Highland Regiment*, ibid, page 59

(17) *A Highland Regiment*, ibid, page 57

And then I find you in the land
Of the unuttered tale.
Then gazing out across the night
I see with glad surmise
The shadows of your loosened hair,
The depths of your grave eyes.

St. Paul's 1912

'. . . the unuttered tale' suggests a very private romance or a figment of the imagination but the last two lines are sufficiently precise to refer to a real person. 'Grave eyes' is less promising than 'bright eyes', or 'loving eyes' and hints at an uncomprehending or unappreciative reaction to his affection.

His romance appears to have begun in the spring or early summer of 1912, when he was nineteen, and still at school.

The poem might represent a late adolescent fantasy, but it is the first of a sequence which traces a first love to its end. It is possible that the love poems relate to a number of loves, but the content of the poems, following the moods of elation, despair, resignation, and defiance, suggest that they are inspired by one romance. The pace at which such matters were conducted by inhibited middle class schoolboys, who had been educated in single sex schools, with no sex education, would make a number of obsessive loves in such a relatively short period unlikely.

There are few clues to her identity: 'loosened hair' might mean someone younger than he was, for girls put their hair up at about eighteen years of age. But 'loosened' is deliberate enough to suggest that she had let her hair down, perhaps someone of his own age, or older, whom he had met on an informal basis. If the girl had Brighton connections Roedean School was just over a mile from his home, although the discipline of the time would make meetings between their girls and local boys highly improbable, if not impossible.

There is little to identify her in the poems in *A Highland Regiment*; the few clues to her whereabouts are in *War, The Liberator*, the posthumous anthology which gathered together most of his unpublished poems. Could the disenchantment with the south in 'Mallaig Bay', and the reference 'when our hearts are bitter' in the 'Return' reflect an early realisation that the girl of his dreams might not be reciprocating his affection? What is certain is that the obsession dominated much of his poetry at Christ Church, and featured in poems written after the outbreak of war.

IN THE NIGHT

Gallant fellows, tall and strong,
Oh, your strength was not for long,
Now within its bed alone
Quite lies your nerveless bone.

Merry maidens, young and fair,
Now your heads are bleached and bare,
Grinning mouths that smiled so sweet,
Buried deep the dancing feet.

Men and maidens fair and brave
Resting in your darkened grave,
Have you left the light behind,
Will you never feel the wind?

Oh I know not if you may,
But from eve till dawn of day
Terror holds me in my bed,
Terror of the living dead.

Oxford, 1912
A Highland Regiment

WANDERER'S DESIRE
TO E.J.S and F.O.T.

I cannot sleep for thinking
    Of things that I have seen
About the highways of the world,
    Where fields are fresh and green,
And hedges lie on either hand
    With a white road between.

I cannot rest for dreaming
    Of the places I have known,
The grasses of the lonely hills,
    The meadows and the sown,
And all the secrets which appear
    To men who walk alone.

The comrades of my walking
    Are calling me to go
And stroll with them across the hills
    Along the road we know,
Past inns where we can drink and talk
    When storm winds bring the snow.

I cannot rise and follow
    The way they're calling me,
So I sit dreaming all the day,
    And all the day I see
The open highways of the world
    Where I would like to be.

Oxford 1913
A Highland Regiment

CAROL OF THE INNOCENTS

As I look out upon the sky
And watch the clouds come driving by,
I know when for a moment's space
I see a laughing baby's face,
It is the Innocents that ride
Across the sky at Christmastide.

Above the world they dance and play,
And they are happy all the day,
And welcome on the joyous morn
A little king among the born.
God looks upon them as they go,
And laughs to see them frolic so.

Their little clouds are stained with red
To show how shamefully they bled,
And all above the world they sing
A carol to their childish king.
It is the Innocents that ride
Across the sky at Christmastide.

Christmas, 1913
A Highland Regiment

SONNET TO THE UNKNOWN LOVE

Across a hundred miles of weary land,
To your dear home by our beloved sea,
I strain my eyes and think I see you stand
The same sweet wonder that you used to be.
I think I see you smile the very way
You had when once we walked across the Downs,
And on the muddy road the palm leaves lay
And the dull trees were garlanded with crowns.

I see the opening of your grave eyes,
And the swift flash when you reveal your heart,
And still between us all this distance lies
Of space and custom keeping us apart,
And still twelve lonely days and nights remain
Ere I shall see and talk to you again.

Undated
War, The Liberator

GROWING PAINS

I

My virtue is gone from me. Nevermore
Shall I see all the flowers and grasses plain,
But only sit and think how I once saw,
And only pray that I may see again.
And in my ears all melody will die,
And on my lips the songs I make will fade,
And I shall only hear in memory
A far – off echo of the songs I made,
And the old happy vision of God's grace,
Where I have mingled with eternal light,
Will comfort me no more, and in its place,
There will be darkness and eternal night;
And faintly in the darkness you will move,
And I shall keep the memory of love.

II

I cannot see your face, I cannot see
The hair back-sweeping from your candid brow,
For night eternal overshadows me,
And eyes that saw you once are sightless now
I cannot hear the music of your voice
That was so beautiful when I could hear,
But only wait upon you and rejoice
To know that in the darkness you are near.
Oh come to me, my dear, and loose my chain,
And with your magic break the evil spell,
And bring me back to light again
To the fair country where I used to dwell.
And now my ears are deaf, my eyes are blind,
And endless darkness gathers in my mind.

III

The end has come for me, the end has come,
The fairies have rung out their silver bell,
And after time will find and leave me dumb
With no more tales of fairyland to tell.
The end has come for me the end of all
Of songs half-uttered and of quick desire,
And hopes that strained to heaven in their fall,
And high dreams fashioned out of clay and fire.
The earth is black about me, and the sun
Is blotted out with darkness overhead,
And there is no hope to comfort me not one,
For love has stolen away, and faith has fled,
And life that once was mine has passed me by,
And I am desolate and shall not die.

IV

There is a city built with walls of gold,
Which is the birthplace of the fairy kings,
Full of strange songs and stories yet untold,
And all the happiness that childhood brings.
The city's gates are open night and day,
And night and day the travellers ride through,
And many that have wandered far away
Would reach again the happy town they knew.
But they can only watch the vision die
And hear the music cease along the strand,
And from the merry dancing – ring no cry
Comes down the falling wind to where they stand,
And so they turn away to try
The darkness of the undiscovered land.

Oxford 1913
A Highland Regiment

DEAD YOUTH

The days of dreams are over,
  The days of songs are done,
So bid good-bye, young lover,
  To boyhood's dying sun;
Good-bye to joy and sadness,
  Good-bye to sun and rain,
And to the swift spring madness
  That will not come again.

Oh days of careless laughter,
  Oh nights of sudden tears,
We shall not know hereafter
  Forgotten hopes and fears.
Oh drams that bide no longer
  With young hearts waxen cold,
Are lovely things no stronger,
  And must you too grow old?

Yes, memory is flying,
  And golden dreams must fade,
And all our loves are dying
  With us beneath the shade;
And buds that ripen never
  Their bloomless leaves have shed,
For youth is dead for ever,
  And all his thoughts are dead.

1913
A Highland Regiment

44

AT THE END

In the dim years, when earth's last sun is setting,
  And all the lamps of heaven are burning low,
Will the gods grant remembrance or forgetting
  Of joys and sorrows that possess us now?

When the day ends and there is no tomorrow,
  Will there be thoughts alive to hurt us yet?
Shall we remember, keeping all our sorrow,
  Or lose our little joys if we forget?

Oh sure, since joy and pain we may not sever,
  Better it is to take the whole alloy,
And keep immortal grief, than lose for ever
  Our slight inheritance of immortal joy.

1913
A Highland Regiment

THE HEARTLESS VOICE

Your voice is like the fairy harps
The wandering shepherd hears,
That tell of laughter without joy,
And light unsaddened tears.

You laugh and I can never tell
If you are glad or no,
You weep and cannot understand
The things that hurt me so.

But still your eager, heartless voice
Is calling night and day,
And I must follow like the men
That hear the fairies play.

1914
A Highland Regiment

45

OLD AGE

In the old years that creep on us so fast,
 When time goes by us with a halting tread,
Shall we sit still and ponder at the last
 The swift years of love that will be dead?
Shall we look back upon the passionate years,
 Where in a maze our younger figures move,
Instinct with half-forgotten hopes and fears,
 And gaze anew on the mirage of love?

Yes, we two, like old actors at a play,
 Watching the beating of a tinsel heart,
Will laugh and weep, and clap our hands, and say,
 'How sadly that young lover played his part
That loved her true and dared not tell her so,
 And she that loved him dared not let him see,'
And we shall watch the hurts of long ago,
 And clap our hands at our old tragedy.

For we shall understand, remembering
 How he spoke thus and she would answer so,
And then we shall see clearly everything
 That was so dark in youth's old puppet-show,
And gazing on the far-off stage where stand
 The misty figures that were you and I,
Each in the darkness will stretch out a hand
 To touch the hand of love before we die.

Oxford, 1914
A Highland Regiment

46

HOPE

Where is the life of springs forgotten,
The happy life of years grown old?
Their bloomless buds are dead and rotten,
The suns that warmed their leaves are cold.
And we that walk the ruined garden
Watch the dry breath of winter harden
In all its beds the barren mould.

Where is the joy of daily meeting
In spring-time when the sun was high?
The winter suns are pale and fleeting,
The gathering clouds o'ercast the sky.
And we that walk alone remember
The fires whose last undying ember
Will burn our hearts until we die.

Oh, heart of youth, too full of sorrow,
Be strong and hold your sorrow fast.
The bitter day and bitter morrow,
That hurt you now, will soon be past.
Winter and spring will end hereafter,
An end in tears, an end of laughter,
And you shall have content at last.

There where the flowers and grasses cover
The lips that laugh, the eyes that weep,
Lover shall meet again with lover,
No man shall break the tryst they keep.
You shall fulfil desire with dreaming
There where all life is inward seeming,
There where the heart of life is sleep.

1914
A Highland Regiment

Alan Mackintosh (centre) at Oxford, 1913 with the 3rd Torpid rowing team (Christ Church)

CHAPTER 2
OXFORD

Lecture-time and my tutor's 'hanker'
Stopping his period's rounded close. . .

'In No Man's Land'
A Highland Regiment

Mackintosh began university studies in October 1912, when he took up his Classics scholarship at Christ Church. Among his contemporaries in Oxford were several ex-Paulines, including Victor Gollancz (at New College) and Edmund Solomon (at Exeter College), both fellow members of the St. Paul's debating society.[1]

Mackintosh was to gain Second Class Honours in Classical Moderations in March 1914,[2] the intermediate examination of his course: this examination came at the end of two years of studying Greek and Latin language and literature. The 'Greats' element of the course which would have filled the next two years was focused on philosophy. Study was not his preoccupation at Oxford. John Murray, his second tutor, mentioned in 'Memoir'[3] that Mackintosh:

> . . . spent two happy years in Oxford. For study, and
> especially the routine study of the schools he cared little.
> Native power and a felicitous exuberance in literary things
> gained him his place in honours classical moderations.

This concurs with the impression of him given by his St Paul's

---

(1) Page 167, 'The Pauline' 1912: 'Oxford letter', anonymous

(2) Christ Church records. Mark Curthoys, archivist

(3) Page 4, 'Memoir', John Murray, in *War, The Liberator*, E. A. Mackintosh, John Lane, The Bodley Head, 1918

teachers: he was intelligent but disinclined to systematic effort. In school effort would have been insisted upon, which would have led to confrontations with the staff. In university, where students were expected to be responsible for themselves, inconsistent effort would be tolerated.

He pursued an interest in politics. This may have been due to his association with Edmund Solomon, who was elected a member of the Oxford Fabian Society on November 16th 1912.

Mackintosh himself subsequently became an Associate of the Society on 22nd February 1913. An Associate was someone in sympathy with the aims of the Society, while not wishing to sign the 'Fabian Basis' and thereby attain full membership.[4] The Fabians were theorists, a powerhouse of ideas, but they were considered remote from the mundane practicalities of day-to-day politics. His association with the Fabians indicates a move from his family's Liberal leanings to the new radical approach to society and politics.

Mackintosh remained an Associate for the rest of his time at Oxford, and Murray mentions in his 'Memoir' that '. . . Mackintosh played with Socialism, to the point of having scruples about the possession of wealth.' This comment is apparently critical. However, though he was not as yet demonstrably committed to a particular stance, this does not mean that Mackintosh was a political dilettante. Since Murray later became Coalition Liberal MP for Leeds West,[5] the comment about Mackintosh 'playing with Socialism' can be seen as an adversarial one.

Mackintosh's first tutor, C.D. Fisher, had been teaching at Oxford for over a decade by the time Mackintosh came to Oxford. This was something of a family tradition, since Fisher's father had been Edward VII's tutor at the university. A former Christ Church student, Fisher was a classicist who read widely in other fields. According to an obituary written by Murray in 1916[6] this reading included:

---

(4) Minutes of the Oxford Fabian Society, 1895-1915. mss top. Oxon. d. 465-466, Dept. of Western Manuscripts, Bodleian Library, Oxford

(5) Page 818, *Who Was Who, 1961-1970*

(6) *Oxford Chronicle* June 1916. Fisher became a private in the R.A.M.C. and spent a year as a driver before joining the Royal Navy. He was a lieutenant on the *Invincible* when the ship was sunk at the Battle of Jutland on May 31st 1916

. . . modern and medieval literatures, English, French
and Italian, and he knew much of France and more of
Italy from long vacation tramps.

Since Murray notes in 'Memoir' Mackintosh's particular enthusiasm for French poetry, it is possible that Fisher played a part in
developing this interest. Murray commented on Fisher's teaching style:

Of his teaching, at once fostering and repressive, and
both in singular degree, it would be hard to say where
the moral discipline ended and that of the intellect and
taste began. Under his eye many of his pupils failed to
make the distinction, encountering in him a compulsive
challenge to clarity and rightness of thought and will for
which the response of nothing less than the whole
personality sufficed.

A hard task master, therefore, yet since Fisher also had: '. . . the
imaginative insight to make his way into very diverse natures, and
a heart big enough for all of them', he would perhaps have found
Mackintosh's quirky individualism rather easier than the teacher
at St. Paul's who had described him as a 'prig'.

John Murray was born at Fraserburgh in 1879, and was educated
at both Aberdeen and Oxford Universities. He noted with interest
Mackintosh's growing interest for Scottish pursuits, particularly
those of the Highlands:[7]

Both in term and out of term he cultivated, above all,
the sentiments and arts of the Highlands. He learned to
play the bagpipes and speak Gaelic, things which later
endeared him to his regiment.

Mackintosh's love of the Highlands was fostered by his father.
Alexander used to take Alan to Teaninich to fish – and salmon used
to arrive in Brighton wrapped in bracken to keep it cool.[8] It is
feasible that he found a piping tutor in London, where Caledonian

---

(7) 'Memoir', ibid, page 4
(8) Family evidence, Rosemary Beazley

societies were strong – piping is difficult to learn, and to have had any real ability would have been the result of persistent effort: it is noteworthy that colleague and author of the informal history of the 5th Seaforths, Captain David Sutherland, makes no mention of Alan Mackintosh as a piper or Gaelic speaker, although he emphasises his role as poet. Perhaps his facility in these was remarkable only in Oxford, where even basic piping and Gaelic speaking would be rare. Or Sutherland may have found these unremarkable attributes in a Highlander. As to Gaelic, apart from employing his intellect in its study, and possibly hiring a tutor, it is clear from his poetry that he had studied Celtic literature and mythology. His visits to the Highlands for walking and fishing holidays would have brought him into contact with native Gaelic speakers, with whom he would have spoken Gaelic.

He had two university companions from Ross-shire. Andrew Knowles Fraser, two years older than Mackintosh, was at Christ College, and Ian MacKenzie, whose roots were in Tain, was at Balliol. Since Mackintosh willed his fishing equipment to Andrew Fraser it is probable that they enjoyed this pastime together in Scotland, where the Fraser family had an estate at Lechmelm, near Ullapool.

Mackintosh's circle was widening and Murray mentions that his friendships were many and ardent.[9] However, there was also a lonely, dark side to Mackintosh's nature. Even while relatively new at Oxford, and in the midst of his studies and other activities he could be profoundly affected by death and attendant morbid thoughts.

The poem 'In The Night',[10] dated Oxford 1912, shows an anxious preoccupation with people who have died in the fullness of their youth. Whether this poem was inspired by the death of a specific friend, or by the prevalence then of death from conditions that are nowadays curable is unknown:

> Terror holds me in my bed,
> Terror of the living dead.

'Terror' may indicate that he had been dreaming about a recently deceased person. The last line shows that he believed in

---

(9) Brighton College archives

(10) *A Highland Regiment*, ibid, page 61

immortality, a theme that emerges in his war poems.

An activity which Mackintosh did enjoy initially was taking long country walks. His companions on such occasions included Edmund Solomon and another friend to whom Mackintosh jointly dedicated a poem, 'Wanderer's Desire'.[11] The second set of initials in the dedication is 'F.O.T.' – Francis Oswald Thorne[12] who, with Mackintosh, was one of the eight occupants of Meadow Buildings staircase 2, during the 1912-1913 academic year. Thorne was also a Classical scholar, had gone up to Oxford in 1911, and was a Pauline. It is noteworthy that Mackintosh 'never shared a set' (a bedroom and a sitting room).[13] This may have contributed to his morose moods.

'Wanderer's Desire' portrays a period when Mackintosh was emotionally very low, and evokes a gulf between the outside world and himself which he is at least temporarily unable to cross, although remaining able to acknowledge the situation:

> So I sit dreaming all the day,
> And all the day I see
> The open highways of the world
> Where I would like to be.

The poem 'Carol of the Innocents', written at Christmas 1913, is an anguished slant on a seasonal theme. It may point to a rejection of the trivialisation of Christmas, which was well under way by then, by reminding people that Christ's birth had immediate serious consequences, or he may simply have been reflecting his own misery: Mackintosh contrasts the horror of the fate of the Innocents slaughtered on Herod's orders with their happy celebration of Christ's birth.[14]

---

(11) *A Highland Regiment* ibid, page 64

(12) Survey of old members, Christ Church 1938. Francis (Frank) Oswald Thorne was born in 1892 and educated at Colet Court and St. Paul's. Joined the Civil Service Rifles in 1914, was commissioned in 13th (Service) Battalion, The Manchester Regiment. Served in France and Mesopotamia. M.C. 1917. Mentioned in dispatches.

(13) Letter from Mark Curthoys, Christ Church, 24.3.1993

(14) *A Highland Regiment*, ibid, page 62

Their little clouds are stained with red
To show how shamefully they bled,
And all above the world they sing
A carol to their childish king.
It is the innocents that ride,
Across the sky at Christmastide.

It is difficult to say what Mackintosh's precise religious beliefs were. Although the pragmatic Non-Conformism of his mother's family would have an influence as he grew up, he was an explorer and self-questioner in this area as in much else, and later seemed to reject the religious norms of his era. He had studied Divinity in school and had to study it for a time at university and pass an exam in it. His name is on the war memorial in St. Columba's United Reformed Church, Oxford, which suggests at least an informal association with the Presbyterian church. This may have been due to his father's upbringing. Mackintosh's radical view may have been coloured by membership of or adherence to the church, in which the Moderator is changed annually, to avoid any hint of élitism, and in which ministers and elders are equals both in individual churches and in the annual assembly. Although not democratic, it was far less hierarchical than the established Church of England.

It is likely that he discussed religious matters with contemporaries like Thorne, who was ordained after the war. Also at Oxford, first as a tutor at Keble College, and then from 1914 at Christ Church, was A.E. (Jack) Rawlinson.[15] Mackintosh and Rawlinson were the only occupants of Tom Quad, staircase 4, during the former's second year at Christ Church, and Rawlinson was nominated as one of Mackintosh's executors. The two were related, as Jack Rawlinson was a grandson of Guinness Rodgers' sister and a Reverend Rawlinson.[16] Both Thorne and Rawlinson became bishops in later life, in Nyasaland and Derby, respectively.

---

(15) Page 909, *Who Was Who, 1951-1960*. Alfred Edward John Rawlinson (1884-1960) was educated at Dulwich College and Corpus Christi College, gaining a First in Classical Moderations, Literae Humaniores and Theology. Ordained in 1909. Student and tutor, Christ Church 1914-1929, Canon Residentiary at Durham, 1929-1936, Bishop Derby, 1936-1959

(16) Family information, Rosemary Beazley

One important thread running through Mackintosh's time at Oxford is featured in several poems written during the period, and may be the explanation for the emotional lows expressed in the previous two poems. The romantic attachment alluded to in 'To the Unknown Love – St. Paul's, 1912' continued to preoccupy him. A poem which should be considered part of this phase, since the distance of separation mentioned is that between Oxford and Brighton, is the similarly titled 'Sonnet to the Unknown Love'. It was not included in his first anthology, *A Highland Regiment*, possibly because the subject would at that time have been identifiable. The separation evoked is social as well as physical:[17]

> Across a hundred miles of weary land,
> To your dear home by our beloved sea. . .
>
> I think I see you smile the very way
> You had when once we walked across the Downs
> And on the muddy road palm branches lay
> And the dull trees were garlanded with crowns.
>
> I see the opening of your grave eyes,
> And the swift flash when you reveal your heart,
> And still between us all this distance lies
> Of space and custom keeping us apart. . .

The relationship was, at least in Mackintosh's mind, still in existence. In 'the swift flash when you reveal your heart' he believes that there was a positive relationship between them, unless he was misinterpreting her thoughts. As the poem was private at that time, and based on the agony of young love, it seems strange that there is no reference to significant words exchanged on previous meetings. They both belonged to a generation schooled to keep their emotions in check, taught to revere or fear the opposite sex, under-informed, and inhibited. If words were restrained then a look, a smile, or a gesture might be the only means of communicating interest. It is clear that he was sure of meeting her, certainly socially, and less probably, on a date.

Had the young people been subject to family disapproval, or

(17) *War, The Liberator*, ibid, page 47

feared they would be? There is a hint of that in 'custom' separating them. Was she unsuitable for social reasons, or religious reasons? Was she high Church of England and he Presbyterian? Or was she Jewish, as were some of his University friends? Or too young, or a relative? The use of 'palm branches' is a way of indicating that the walk across the Downs took place at Easter.

In other poems he agonises and tries to retrieve what seems to have ended. At times his anguished moods show a mental and emotional malaise which may have been more than just the effects of thwarted love.

In 'Growing Pains',[18] a poem of four sonnet-length stanzas which is his most sustained effort to that date, if the arrangement of *A Highland Regiment* is chronological, Mackintosh recounts the desolation of spirit which is overpowering him – even creative and religious comforts are temporarily out of reach: in it he expresses his need for the love that has receded:

> And faintly in the darkness you will move,
> And I shall keep the memory of love.

He feels imprisoned by increasing mental suffering and traumatised senses, crying out to be rescued by the woman who is the object of his love:

> And bring me back into the light again
> To the fair country where I used to dwell
> And now my ears are deaf, my eyes are blind,
> And endless darkness gathers in my mind.

The last stanza echoes 'The Kingdom of the Downs' in speaking of a longed-for place which now, instead of being a remote but attainable embodiment of dreams which can and must be retained, is an idyll impossibly out of his reach; the only remaining alternative is to strike out into the present darkness:

> And many that have wandered far away
> Would reach again the happy town they knew.

---

(18) *A Highland Regiment*, ibid, page 66

His preoccupation with darkness and hopelessness is akin to grief. He is inconsolable and sees no hope. In 'Dead Youth', dated 1913, as in 'Growing Pain', he bids goodbye to the turbulence of the romance with apparent finality:[19]

Good-bye to joy and sadness,
Good-bye to sun and rain,
And to the swift spring madness
That will not come again.

He then uses the image of prematurely halted growth to denote the culmination of his fruitless youth, or possibly even the fruitlessness of their relationship, and implies that his thought processes had temporarily ceased:

And buds that ripen never
Their bloomless leaves have shed,
For youth is dead for ever
And all his thoughts are dead.

Mackintosh is eventually able to view with some equanimity and objectivity the prospect of looking back at his current predicament, and in 'At The End' has reached the point of feeling that eliminating the prospect of pain would take away also the possibility of joy, since the two are often inextricably joined in the human experience: he is just beginning to recall the happiness of the romance through his pain at the loss of it:[20]

Oh sure, since joy and pain we may not sever,
Better it is to take the whole alloy,
And keep immortal grief, than lose for ever
Our slight inheritance of immortal joy.

By the following year, in the poem 'Old Age', Mackintosh is surveying the romance from the imagined far-distant future, when

---

(19) *A Highland Regiment*, ibid, page 72
(20) *A Highland Regiment*, ibid, page 74

both parties might be able to look back on it together as if they
were the audience in a play:[21]

> And then we shall see clearly everything
> That was so dark in youth's old puppet show,
> And gazing on the far-off stage where stand
> The misty figures that were you and I,
> Each in the darkness will stretch out a hand
> To touch the hand of love before we die.

The implication of resolution inherent in both of them being
present on this occasion is countered by the unreality of the
situation: Mackintosh has distanced himself, both in time and by
being an observer, from the hurt he has been through. His ability
to imagine himself in old age, reviewing his youth after a lifetime
of experience, and to predict a real or metaphorical looking back
together at their young romance, is the first evidence of a device
that he later adopts in 'Peace Upon Earth' in 1916 (see Chapter 5).
It is a position rare in someone so young, that of realising that time
would create emotional detachment and healing. The notion that
there would be a clarity in their recollection, as distinct from
'everything that was so dark in youth's old puppet show' suggests
that neither of them had been able to express themselves successfully
in their meetings, which is often the case in youthful romances.

Mackintosh was obsessive, angry and deeply hurt: where others
might have sought consolation in drink, physical exercise or in
superficial affairs, he did not. The impression is of someone to
whom the advice 'there are plenty more fish in the sea' would have
fallen on deaf ears.

Featuring the blighted growth seen in 'Dead Youth', the poem
'Hope'[22] returns to less gentle imagery:

> Where is the life of Springs forgotten,
> The happy life of years grown old?
> Their bloomless buds are dead and rotten,
> The suns that warmed their leaves are cold.

---

(21) A Highland Regiment, ibid, page 88
(22) A Highland Regiment, ibid, page 91

The title is ironic, since there is no comfortable and sentimental end in view. Though lovers will be together at the end, this will only be the finality of death in the 'ruined garden' of the graveyard, and he implies that there was intervention to keep them apart in:

No man shall break the tryst they keep.

If Mackintosh had not been a student, but had been in necessary and engrossing employment, he may not have become such a victim of despair. Mackintosh lashes out much more bitterly in 'The Heartless Voices', in which he rails against his loved one's lack of real feeling and empathy:[23]

You weep and cannot understand
The things that hurt me so.

The domination of his writing by poems mourning unrequited love was not total. John Murray saw much promise in a verse play written by Mackintosh while at Oxford. 'The Remembered Gods'[24] is in the style of a Greek tragedy, a form familiar to Mackintosh through his years of classical education, but it is set in the world of his Celtic ancestors. There is much in it concerning the tension between the influence of the ancient Gods and more recent Christianity, an aspect of the Scottish psyche which was evidently of great interest to him: he may have been immersed in the literature of the Celtic Twilight School, of which W.B.Yeats, William Sharp and William Black, who died in Brighton in 1898, were leading exponents:

The gods are living yet, and have their thrones
In the invisible desires of men.
Below the quiet current of our lives
They move and labour to destroy the chains
Your saints have cast upon our memory.

---

(23) *A Highland Regiment*, ibid, page 90

(24) *War, The Liberator*, ibid, page 53

Still in our hearts the ancient fires burn high,
And Balor, tempest armoured, calls to us.
And you with gentle prayer and song adore
Your pitiful, sad song the whole day long.

Alastair, the character speaking above, is described as a 'young stranger' in the listing at the beginning of the play. It is possible to see Alastair as a representation of Mackintosh's own personal exploration of belief. Alastair goes on to pose the following question:

But in the echoing nights when none is by,
In the lone nights do they not burn you still?

This gives an indication of Mackintosh's thinking, but also shows an eerie, brooding mood which is comparable to those under-pinning many other of his poems. However, though he showed in his writing a propensity for dark moods and a sense of being apart, he did retain a wide circle of friends, and Murray included in 'Memoir' an assessment which describes the outgoing nature of Mackintosh's character:

His roving eye, merry, tender, cautious, penetrating,
bold by rapid turns, epitomised the richness of his
nature and his still rarer force of self-expression.

Murray's 'Memoir' was to a dead hero. It is unlikely that he would have written anything to offend. 'Roving eye' would not mean having an eye for the girls, but that Mackintosh was a constant observer of the human scene. Murray recognises mischievous humour, which is confirmed by those who came to know him in the army. 'Tender' and 'cautious' imply sensitivity and reticence, the antithesis of his merriness and his boldness. His boldness by 'rapid turns' may echo his 'occasional lapses of taste' referred to in his December 1911 school report (see Chapter 1) – a propensity to shock his elders, which would not have been difficult in his era.

Mackintosh was not an athlete – there is no record of partici-pation in sport at school. Apart from walking and fishing in Scotland, and going for long walks with his friends in Oxford, his only sporting interest was in rowing. At Christ Church he rowed for the Third Torpid[25] – 'toggers',[26] an eight. Until 1870 a Torpid was a college's second boat, but after that date the Torpids took part in a separate competition, in the Hilary or Lent term. The Eights were rowed in the Trinity (summer) term, and university oarsmen would not row in the Torpids. Then, as now,the Torpids would include students who were not serious athletes, and were rowing for fun. As there was no record of his participation in any other sporting activities in surviving club minutes, the Third Torpid would appear to represent the pinnacle of his sporting endeavour at Oxford.

A photograph of the 1913 Third Torpid gives a rare impression of Mackintosh at university, seated confidently amidst his rowing friends. The team photograph[27] lists the names of nine of the ten men present, in no discernible order, but notes their weights and places in the boat: Mackintosh weighed 10 stones 11 lbs and was stroke. Amongst the group is Adolph Marschall von Bieberstein, a German diplomat's son, who was to gain the Iron Cross in the war that destroyed their generation.

Mackintosh was later to look back on university life with much affection. In 'Oxford From The Trenches', written at Bécourt in 1915, he was to include these lines:[28]

Memory is on me of the warm dim chambers,
And the laughter of my friends in the huge high-ceilinged hall,
Lectures and the voices of the dons deep droning,
The things that were so common once
– Oh God, I feel them all.

---

(25) Christ Church Records
(26) Letter from Geoffrey Dearmer to the authors, 22.2.94: 'I, too, rowed in 'toggers' or Torpids.'
(27) Christ Church archives
(28) *A Highland Regiment*, ibid, page 24

ANNS AN GLEANN'SAN ROBH MI OG

In the glen when I was young
Blue-bell stems stood close together,
In the evenings dew-drops hung
Clear as glass above the heather.
I'd be sitting on a stone,
Legs above the water swung,
I a laddie all alone,
In the glen when I was young.

Well, the glen is empty now,
And far am I from those that love me,
Water to my knees below,
Shrapnel in the clouds above me;
Watching till I sometimes see,
Instead of death and fighting men,
The people that were kind to me,
And summer in the little glen.

Hold me close until I die,
Lift me up, it's better so;
If, before I go, I cry,
It isn't I'm afraid to go;
Only sorry for the boy
Sitting there with legs aswung
In my little glen of joy,
In the glen where I was young.

August 1914
A Highland Regiment

CHA TIL MACCRUIMEIN
(Departure of the 4th Camerons)

The pipes in the street were playing bravely,
    The marching lads went by,
With merry hearts and voices singing
    My friends marched out to die;
But I was hearing a lonely pibroch
    Out of an older war,
'Farewell, farewell, farewell, MacCrimmon,
    MacCrimmon comes no more.'

And every lad in his heart was dreaming
    Of honour and wealth to come,
And honour and noble pride were calling
    To the tune of the pipes and the drum;
But I was hearing a woman singing
    On dark Dunvegan shore,
'In battle of peace, with wealth or honour,
    MacCrimmon comes no more.'

And there in front of the men were marching,
    With feet that made no mark,
The grey old ghosts of the ancient fighters
    Come back again from the dark;
And in front of them all MacCrimmon piping
    A weary tune and sore,
'On the gathering day, for ever and ever,
    MacCrimmon comes no more.'

Bedford, 1915
A Highland Regiment

TO A DEAD SOLDIER

So I shall never see you more.
The northern winds will blow in vain
Brave and heart-easing off the shore.
You will not sail with them again.
I shall not see you wait for me
Where the beach and the dulse is brown,
Nor hear at night across the sea
Your chorus of the Nighean doun.

Are you so easy handled now
That Flanders soil can keep you still
Although the northern breezes blow
All day across the fairy hill?
And can an alien lowland clay
Hold fast your soul and body too,
Or will you rise and come away
To where our friendship waits for you?

You cannot rest so far from home,
Your heart will miss the northern wind,
Back from the lowland fields will come,
Your soul the grave can never bind.
Once more your hands will trim the sail
That carries us across the bay
To where the summer islands pale
Over the seas and far away.

And you will sail and watch with me
The things we saw and loved before,
The happy islands of the sea,
The breakers white against the shore.
A hundred joys that we held dear
Will call you from the Flanders town,
And in the evenings I shall hear
Your chorus of the Nighean doun.

Bedford, 1915
A Highland Regiment

CHRIST IN FLANDERS

Oh, you that took our sin and pain
Upon your shoulders long ago,
Are you come back to earth again,
About the battle do you go?
By trenches where with bitter cries
Men's spirits leave their tortured clay,
Oh, wanderer with the mournful eyes,
Are you on Flanders soil today?

The battle fog is wreathed and curled
Before us, that we cannot see
The darkness of the newer world
As your eternal agony,
The gallant hearts, the bitter blood,
The pains of them that have not died,
A bright light in the eyes of God
A sharp spear-point in his side.

> Church parade, 1915
> *A Highland Regiment*

THE WAITING WIFE

Out on a hillside the wild birds crying,
A little low wind and the white clouds flying,
A little low wind from the southward blowing,
What should I know of its coming and going?

Over the battle the shrapnel crying
A tune of lament for the dead and dying,
A little low wind that is moaning and weeping
For the mouths that are cold and the brave hearts sleeping.

I and my man were happy together
In the summer days and warm June weather –
What is the end of our laughter and singing?
A little low wind from the southward winging.

The hearth is cold and my house is lonely,
And nothing for me but waiting only,
Feet round the house that come into it never,
And a voice in the wind that is silent for ever.

Golspie, 1915
A Highland Regiment

FROM A WAR STATION.
To A.K.F.

In Oxford now the lamps are lit,
   The city bells ring low,
And up and down the silent town
   The ghosts of friendship go.

With whispering laughs they meet and pass
   As we were used to do,
And somewhere in the airy crowd
   My spirits walk with you.

The troopers quarter in the rooms
   That once were yours and mine,
And you are lying out to-night
   Behind the firing-line.

But still in rooms that were our own
   We wander, you and I,
And night and day our spirits walk
   Along the empty High.

Golspie, 1915
A Highland Regiment

To Edward and Ivy Forsyth

Darlings (if I may call you so)
I fear that I can only sing
Of sorrows that your elders know.
So you I send a better thing.

O may you journey many a day
Across the great Gromboolean plain,
Because, when I was far away,
You came and brought me back again.

Because, when darkness covered me,
You came and took me by the hand,
And opened my blind eyes to see
The little hills of Fairyland.

Ewart Alan Mackintosh
16 Sussex Square
Brighton.

VERSES TO TWO CHILDREN
(With a Copy of Lear's 'Nonsense Rhymes')

Darlings, if I may call you so,
   I fear that I can only sing
Of sorrows that your elders know.
   To you I send a better thing. . .

Oh may you wander many a day
   Across the great Gromboolian plain,
Because, when I was far away,
   You came and brought me back again.

Because, when darkness covered me,
   You came and took me by the hand,
And opened my blind eyes to see
   The little hills of Fairyland.

Brora, 1912
A Highland Regiment

MATRI ALMAE

City of hopes and golden dreaming
   Set with a crown of tall grey towers,
City of mist that round you streaming
   Screens the vision of vanished hours,
All the wisdom of youth far-seeing,
   All the things that we meant to do,
Dreams that will never be clothed in being,
   Mother, your sons have left with you.

Clad in beauty of dreams begotten
   Strange old city for ever young,
Keep the vision that we've forgotten,
   Keep the songs we have never sung.
So shall we hear your music calling,
   So from a land where songs are few
When the shadows of life are falling,
   Mother, your sons come back to you.

So with the bullets above us flying,
   So in the midst of horror and pain
We shall come back from the sorrow of dying
   To wander your magical ways again.
For that you keep and grow not older
   All the beauty we ever knew,
As the fingers of death grow colder,
   Mother, your sons come back to you.

In the Leave Train, 1915
A Highland Regiment

THE LAST MEETING

Last time you met me shadowed white,
   A very queen for stateliness,
And all the jewels of the night
   Were tangled in your ivory dress.
Your eyes were strange, your lovely smile
   As though we never met before –
I saw you such a little while
   Who shall not see you evermore.

God knows the gates were strong between,
   But still my trumpet might have blown
Had you not looked so great a queen,
   Had I but seen you all alone.
But there we sat the dinner through
   And talked like strangers of the war.
I only spoke an hour with you,
   Who now shall speak with you no more.

Maybe I waited over-long,
   You spoke no word to tell me so.
Perhaps the gates might be too strong
   For any blast that I could blow –
Ah well, it hardly matters now,
   My whispering ghost drifts through the rain,
The shroud of death is at my brow,
   I shall not come to you again.

1915
A Highland Regiment

HARVEST

Along the dusty highway,
And through the little town,
The people of the country
Are riding up and down.
Behind the lines of fighting
They gather in all day
The harvest, folk are reaping
At home and far away.

If on the hills around us,
Where now the thrush sings low,
The face of earth were bitter,
It would not hurt us so.
Though earth grew strange and savage
And all the world were new,
It would not tear our memory
The way the cornfields do.

Oh, you that fought your battles
Beneath the Southern Cross,
The earth was kinder to you,
You could not feel your loss,
Nor waken every morning
And clear before you see
The grassy fields and meadows
Where you would wish to be.

But in a haunted corn-land
We move, as in a dream
Of quiet hills and hedges
And a swift flowing stream,
And on the hills about us
Through all the din of war,
The home that we were born in,
And we shall see no more.

Buire-sur-Ancre, 1915
A Highland Regiment

OXFORD FROM THE TRENCHES

The clouds are in the sky, and a light rain falling,
And through the sodden trench splashed figures come and go,
But deep in my heart are the old years calling,
And memory is on me of the things I used to know.

Memory is on me of the warm dim chambers,
And the laughter of my friends in the huge high-ceilinged hall,
Lectures and the voices of the dons deep-droning,
The things that were so common once – O God, I feel them all.

Here are the great things, life and death and danger,
All I ever dreamed of in the days that used to be,
Comrades and good-fellowship, the soul of an army,
But, oh, it is the little things that take the heart of me.

For all we knew of old, for little things and lovely,
We bow us to a greater life beyond our hope or fear,
To bear its heavy burdens, endure its toils unheeding,
Because of all the little things so distant and so dear.

Bécourt, 1915
A Highland Regiment

THE UNDYING RACE

Here in the narrow broken way
   Where silently we go,
Steadfast above their valiant clay
   Forgotten crosses show.
Our whispers call to many a ghost
   Across the flare-light pale,
And from their graves the Breton host
   Stand up beside the Gael.

Year upon year of ancient sleep
   Have rusted on our swords,
But once again our place we keep
   Against the Saxon hordes.
Since Arthur ruled in Brittany,
   And all the world was new,
The fires that burned our history,
   Burn in our spirits too.

One speech beyond their memory
   Binds us together still,
One dream of home wherein we see
   River and sea and hill.
When in the night-time Fingal's peers
   Fight their old wars again,
The blood of twice two thousand years
   Leaps high in every vein.

Old songs that waked King Arthur's knights
   Stir in our memory yet,
Old tales of olden heroes fights
   That we cannot forget,
To die as Fingal's warriors died
   The great men long ago,
Breton and Gael stand side by side
   Against the ancient foe.

La Boisselle, 1915
A Highland Regiment

THE SMOKE HELMET
(three of six verses)

Tune – 'Lum Hat wantin' a Croon'

The O.C. for his Subaltern sent,
Who was standing, and looking forlorn,
And he told him at once to make out a Report,
Stating reasons of any and every sort,
Why MacKay's Smoke Helmet was torn.

So the Subaltern sat up all night,
Till he wished he had never been born,
And sent a report to the angry C.O.,
Stating seventy probable reasons or so,
Why MacKay's smoke helmet was torn.

From Brigade to Division it went,
And made General Headquarters to mourn,
And the Master of Ordnance made an Indent,
And a hundred and twenty Smoke Helmets were sent
For the one that Mackay had torn.

War, The Liberator

FOUR AND TWENTY BOMBERS

Tune – 'The Ball of Kirriemuir'

Oh, four and twenty bombers,
Gaed out at La Boiseselle,
An' only ane cam back again,
Remarkin' it was hell.

Chorus –
Singing 'Wha'll dae't the next time?
Wha'll dae'it the noo?
The lads that did it last time
Cannae dae it noo.'

We bombed 'em for four hours,
Until we had tae stop,
An' then there was a row o' duds
Upon the crater top.

Chorus –
Singing, etc.

Sae here's tae the Kaiser,
We'll soon hae's blood
If we cannae throw a live
We can aye buzz a dud

Chorus –
Singing, etc.

This choice lyric, from which the last verse is omitted, for
obvious reasons, is set to an ancient and disreputable Scotch
ballad. (Mackintosh's note)

War, The Liberator

IN NO MAN'S LAND

The hedge on the left, and the trench on the right,
And the whispering, rustling wood between,
And who knows where in the wood tonight,
Death or capture may lurk unseen,
The open field and the figures lying
Under the shade of the apple trees –
Is it the wind in the branches sighing
Or a German trying to stop a sneeze.

Louder the voices of night come thronging,
But over them all the sound is clear,
Taking me back to the place of my longing
And the cultured sneezes I used to hear,
Lecture-time and my tutor's 'hanker'
Stopping his period's rounded close,
Like the frozen hand of a German ranker
Down in a ditch with a cold in his nose.

I'm cold too, and a stealthy shuffle
From the man with a pistol covering me,
And the Bosche moving off with a snap and a shuffle
Break the windows of memory –
I can't make sure till the moon gets lighter –
Anyway, shooting is over bold,
Oh, damn you, get back to your trench, you blighter,
I really can't shoot a man with a cold.

Hammerhead Wood, Thiepval, 1915
A Highland Regiment

SNOW IN FRANCE

The tattered grass of No Man's Land
   Is white with snow today,
And up and down the deadly slopes
   The ghosts of childhood play.

The sentries, peering from the line,
   See in the tumbled snow
Light forms that were their little selves
   A score of years ago.

We look and see the crumpled drifts
   Piled in a little glen,
And you are back in Saxony
   And children once again.

From joyous hand to laughing face
   We watch the snow-balls fly,
The way we used ere we were men
   Waiting our turn to die.

Tonight across the empty slopes
   The shells will scream once more,
And flares go up and bullets fly
   The way they did before;

But for a little space of peace
   We watch them come and go,
The children that were you and I
   At play among the snow.

Bois d'Authuille, 1915
A Highland Regiment

BEFORE THE SUMMER

When our men are marching lightly up and down,
When the pipes are playing through the little town,
I see a thin line swaying through wind and mud and rain
And the broken regiments come back to rest again.

Now the pipes are playing, now the drums are beat,
Now the strong battalions are marching up the street,
But the pipes will not be playing and the bayonets will not shine,
When the regiments I dream of come stumbling down the line.

Between the battered trenches their silent dead will lie
Quiet with grave eyes staring at the summer sky.
There is a mist upon them so that I cannot see
The faces of my friends that walk the little town with me.

Lest we see a worse thing than it is to die,
Live ourselves and see our friends cold beneath the sky,
God grant we too be lying there in wind and mud and rain
Before the broken regiments come stumbling back again.

Corbie, 1916
A Highland Regiment

Rosemary Beazley

Trench warfare, early 1916. Mackintosh is third from the left

CHAPTER 3
WAR

And once again our place we keep
Against the Saxon hordes.

'The Undying Race'
A Highland Regiment

The outbreak of war on 3rd August 1914 unleashed a tide of patriotic fervour. Recruiting offices were mobbed by men of all ages and classes, and university Officers Training Corps, through their Boards of Military Studies, were commissioning young men who had the minimum necessary military qualifications, acquired through school or university cadet corps. Others with no military qualifications whatsoever pulled strings to obtain commissions and trained for their role on the job.

Alan Mackintosh anticipated his future in the army when he wrote *Anns an Gleann'san robh mi og* ('In the glen when I was young') in August 1914:[1]

Well, the glen is empty now,
And far am I from those that love me. . .

Francis Thorne enlisted in the 15th Battalion of the London Regiment (Civil Service Rifles) T.F. (Territorial Forces) and was later commissioned in the 13th (Service) Battalion of The Manchester Regiment.[2] Edmund Solomon joined the 4th Royal West Kent Regiment T.F., from which he was subsequently commissioned in the Royal Marine Light Infantry.[3] Andrew Fraser was commissioned in

---

(1) Page 13, *A Highland Regiment*, E.A.Mackintosh.

(2) Christ Church Survey of Old Members. 1938

(3) Register of Exeter College, Oxford, 1891-1921

the 4th (Ross Highland Battalion) Seaforth Highlanders T.F.[4] Its G Company had headquarters at Alness, Mackintosh's ancestral home.

Mackintosh was rejected because of bad eyesight.[5] If his eyesight was such that the army would not initially accept him, it suggests he must have worn spectacles, but they do not appear in photographs of him. Like many officers at the time he chose to wear pince-nez spectacles, and these are evident in a cartoon drawn in 1917 by one of his officer cadets.[6] Their inclusion in the cartoon indicates that he wore them regularly; that he did not wear them in photographs as late as 1917 suggests that he was sensitive about his image.

The effect on his morale of his rejection must have been devastating, but he persisted and marked time for four months in Brighton and Oxford. He served in the Oxford University Officers Training Corps, but whether he had been in it before the war, or joined in August to strengthen his case for a commission, is unknown. His commission was finally announced in the *London Gazette* on 1st January 1915:

> 5th (The Sutherland and Caithness Battalion) Seaforth
> Highlanders (Ross-shire Buffs, the Duke of Albany's).
> Cadet Ewart Alan Mackintosh, from the Oxford University
> Contingent, Senior Division, Officers Training Corps, to be
> Second Lieutenant. Dated 31st December 1914.

Given that his friend Andrew Fraser was in the 4th Seaforths and that Mackintosh ended his military career in the same battalion, it is possible that his gazetting to the 5th Seaforths was not his first choice and that he might have preferred his county battalion.

The 5th Seaforth Highlanders was a Territorial Force battalion, whose companies were based at Golspie, Dornoch, Bonar Bridge, Brora, Thurso, Wick, Halkirk and Castletown, with subsidiary drill stations in the outlying areas of each of these centres. Unlike the other Seaforth Highlander battalions, which wore Mackenzie tartan

---

(4) Letter to John MacLennan from Mr. Fraser, 1974

(5) Introduction by Coningsby Dawson in later edition of *War, The Liberator*, E.A.Mackintosh. John Lane, The Bodley Head, 1918

(6) Page 49, 'Graduating in Arms' No. 2 Officers Cadet Battalion, Cambridge, 1917

and the stag's head badge, the 5th Battalion wore Sutherland tartan, and the cat's badge of the Sutherland clan, with the motto *Sans Peur* ('Without Fear') on the belt encircling the cat. Officers' badges had silver feathers, the number of which designated their rank: second lieutenants had one.

Mackintosh joined the battalion at Bedford, where it had been sent in August 1914, when the 1/1st Highland Division, of which it was part, was mobilised. It trained there until the division went overseas in early May 1915, renumbered the 51st (Highland) Division. Mackintosh was not destined to go with them: like most Territorial battalions the 5th Seaforths had formed duplicate battalions, thus there was a 1/5th Battalion and a 2/5th Battalion. Territorials had enlisted before the war for home defence only, and the 1/5th was composed of those who had volunteered for overseas service, were trained, and were physically fit.

The 2/5th Battalion had been formed at Golspie of men who did not have these qualifications: to these were added soldiers of the same categories who had gone south to Bedford in August 1914, or had been sent there after enlisting. The 2/5th never went to France: it trained drafts for France.

Mackintosh was in Bedford in February 1915, when three battalions of the Highland Division were sent to France. One of these drew men from mainland Inverness-shire, and from the islands of Skye, Harris and North Uist, which were largely Gaelic-speaking areas. For them Mackintosh created *Cha Till Maccruimen* – 'Departure of the 4th Camerons':[7]

> With merry hearts and voices singing,
> My friends went out to die.
>
> And there in front of the men were marching,
> With feet that made no mark,
> The grey old ghosts of the ancient fighters,
> Come back again from the dark.

The rhythm is that of the old Gaelic poem, *Cha Till Maccruimen*, and the last lines of each verse are verbatim translations from Gaelic. The MacCrimmons had been the pipers of the MacLeods of

---

(7) *A Highland Regiment*, ibid, page 16

Dunvegan and had run the *piobaireachd* (pibroch) college at Boreraig in Skye, and their piping skill had been unsurpassed. One legend had it that the last MacCrimmon piper played his way into a fairy cave and was never seen again: another says that a MacCrimmon piper accurately prophesied his own death in the Jacobite Rising of 1745-1746. The analogy with the likely fate of the 4th Cameron Highlanders is clear, and by the end of the autumn of 1915 they had been so badly reduced that in March 1916 the survivors had been absorbed into the 1st Camerons.[8]

Mackintosh's use of rhythm, whether from the poetry of the Highlands, or from his piping experience, confirms his knowledge of Highland culture.

In 'To a Dead Soldier',[9] also written at Bedford, his belief in immortality is evident, and he subscribes to the Highland assertion that souls would always find their way back to their own homelands: this is best known in the air 'The Bonnie Banks of Loch Lomond' where 'you'll take the high road, and I'll take the low' refers to the living going home normally and the dead souls making their way home below ground.

The summer islands of which he writes would be the Summer Isles, off Ullapool, seen in his youthful travels to holiday with Andrew Fraser at Lechmelm, near Ullapool: the *Nighean doun* (nee-an down) is a reference to the song: 'Ho ro, my nut brown maiden'. He writes of a soldier killed in Flanders:

> Back from the lowland fields will come,
> Your soul the grave can never bind.
> Once more your hands will trim the sail
> That carries us across the bay
> To where the summer islands pale
> Over the sea and far away.
> And in the evening I shall hear
> Your chorus of the Nighean Doun.

'Christ in Flanders'[10] was prompted by attendance at a church

---

(8) Page 103, British Regiments 1914-1918, Brigadier E.A.James, OBE Samson Books

(9) *A Highland Regiment*, ibid, page 18

(10) *A Highland Regiment*, ibid, page 21

parade in 1915. These parades were compulsory for officers and men, and the theology took a conventional, conservative and often ferociously patriotic form. Mackintosh echoes this, especially in the first and fourth lines, where he recognises Christ as the atoner of humanity's sins, and seems to accept the concept of a second coming:

> Oh, you who took our sin and pain
> Upon your shoulders long ago,
> Are you come back to earth again,
> About the battle do you go?

By March of 1915 Mackintosh was in the small town of Golspie,[11] headquarters of the 1/5th Seaforths, training with the 2/5th Seaforths, which, with 2/4th and 2/6th Seaforths, and the 2/4th Camerons, would become the 191st Brigade of the 64th (2nd Highland) Division, with a home defence and reinforcement role.

'The Waiting Wife',[12] written at Golspie, makes less of immortality than 'To a Dead Soldier', maybe because it was written from observation of the sharp reality of recent widowhood, rather than from his imagination: there is less of the optimistic and consolatory belief in immortality found in 'To a Dead Soldier' and more of the misery of grief:

> The hearth is cold and my house is lonely,
> And nothing for me but waiting only,
> Feet round the house that come into it never,
> And a voice in the wind that is silent for ever.

While at Golspie he visited a Mrs. Forsyth and her children, Ivy and Edward, five miles away, in the village of Brora. Mackintosh enjoyed the children's company, and Miss Ivy Forsyth recalled 'my mother was an attractive young widow and I think that may have been an extra reason for his visits.'[13] Her husband had been a doctor, who had died of pneumonia.

He sent the children a copy of Lear's *Nonsense Rhymes* inscribed

---

(11) *British Regiments 1914-1918*, ibid, page 103

(12) *A Highland Regiment*, ibid, page 20

(13) Letter from Ivy Forsyth to authors, 1993

with 'Verses to Two Young Children'.[14] The anthology version of
the poem is quoted below, but the flyleaf version as photo-copied
by Ivy Forsyth to the authors has the phrase 'if I may call you so' in
brackets.

Does this poem stem from sorrows inspired by his lost love,
Mrs. Forsyth's widowhood, or the war? The lost love would appear
to be the most likely as he thanks the children for opening his blind
eyes to see the little hills of Fairyland – a restoration of the innocence of childhood that had vanished with the end of his romance:

> Darlings, if I may call you so,
> I fear that I can only sing
> Of sorrows that your elders know. . .
>
> Because, when darkness covered me,
> You came and took me by the hand,
> And opened my blind eyes to see
> The little hills of Fairyland.

The poem is dated 1912 in *A Highland Regiment*, yet Ivy Forsyth
remembers him meeting her family when they lived in Brora in
1915 'very close to where he was stationed in Golspie',[15] which
suggests that the poem was written in 1915 at the earliest. Either
the date was misprinted in *A Highland Regiment*, which is unlikely,
as Mackintosh corrected the proofs, or he possibly changed it. Was
this to maintain the sequence of love, obsession, hurt, despair and
defiance which runs through his ordering of his love poems in *A
Highland Regiment*, so that the unknown love would not know that
he was still hurting in 1915? Or was the date altered to avoid
involving Mrs. Forsyth? This is akin to not publishing 'Sonnet to
an Unknown Love' in *A Highland Regiment*. Ivy Forsyth wrote in 1993:

> Although it is such a long time ago I remember how kind
> Lieutenant Mackintosh was to my mother and us children.
> . . for me he is a lovely memory of my childhood.[16]

---

(14) *A Highland Regiment*, ibid, page 60. Letter from Ivy Forsyth,
and her copy of the flyleaf

(15) Letter from Ivy Forsyth, ibid

(16) Letter from Ivy Forsyth, ibid

Mrs Forsyth, Ivy and Edward, visited by Mackintosh at Brora

Ivy Forsyth

Ivy Forsyth was nine or ten years old when she met him.

At Golspie he dedicated a poem to Andrew Fraser, who had landed in France with the 4th Seaforths on 7th November 1914:[17]

Oxford is a recurring theme in his poetry. In the dark winter weather of Golspie, Oxford would be appealing to him for itself, not just for its friendly associations. The poem: 'From a War Station. To A. K. F.'[18] is populated with ghosts, as was much of his poetry – not menacing ghosts, simply the shadows of times past, or the shadows of the future's past:

> And up and down the silent town,
> The ghosts of friendship go.

---

(17) *British Regiments 1914-1918*, ibid, page 103

(18) *A Highland Regiment*, ibid, page 15

In April 1915 the 2/5th Seaforths moved with their brigade to Fort George, which was overcrowded with the 10th Seaforths and other reinforcements.[19] It is likely that they moved to a camp in the Carse of Ardersier, with 2/4th Seaforths. The battalion remained there until their brigade left Fort George in July, to continue training at Blair Atholl, Perthshire.

Towards the end of July Mackintosh was on embarkation leave, knowing that he was to join the 5th Seaforths, with the 51st (Highland) Division, somewhere in France. In a leave train in 1915 he wrote 'Matri Almae',[20] again recalling Oxford. In the penultimate line he recognises that Oxford's sons may never live to attain their student dreams.

> All the things we meant to do,
> Dreams that will never be clothed in being,
> Mother your sons have left with you.

The same recognition of the risk of death in France is in the last lines of a poem in which he recorded seeing the 'unknown love' in 1915: 'Last Meeting'.[21] The poem is not precisely dated as that would have identified the girl to readers at the gathering at which they met – but the meeting may have been on his embarkation leave, for he finishes the last verse:

> Ah, well, it hardly matters now,
> My whispering ghost drifts through the rain,
> The shroud of death is at my brow,
> I shall not come to you again.

Many a young man going to war would have the anticipatory excitement of going overseas reinforced by the knowledge that he had the support of a sweetheart as well as his family, who would write to him, send parcels, and be there for him on his return. The situation Mackintosh describes is one of loneliness and fatalism,

---

(19) British Regiments 1914-1918 ibid, page 103, and Queen's Own Highlander magazine

(20) *A Highland Regiment*, ibid, page 35

(21) *A Highland Regiment*, ibid, page 93

which would only heighten his concern at the risks that awaited him in France.

Less poetically, on July 28th, 1915, he signed his will:[22]

> . . . to my sister Muriel Mackintosh all my worldly goods
> save and except twenty pounds each to my niece and
> nephew and my books to Edmund John Solomon of 47
> Rowan Road Green, Hammersmith and the Royal Marine
> Light Infantry and my rods and fishing tackle to Andrew
> Knowles Fraser of Leek [Lech] Melm House in the County
> of Ross-shire and the Seaforth Highlanders and I direct
> that my said sister Muriel Mackintosh shall publish all my
> poems in the order in which I have left them. . .

The poems to which he referred were all his pre-war and pre-France poems (except those later found in *War, The Liberator*) and 'Return', from the Pauline. He appointed his sister Lilian Mackintosh, 16 Sussex Square, Brighton, and his second year university neighbour, the Rev. A.E.J. Rawlinson, clerk in Holy Orders, Christ Church, as his executors.

The Highland Division was then near Albert, on the Somme, where it was taking over the front line from the French, who had held a disproportionately large part of it whilst the British assembled a continental sized army for the first time in their history. Some of the following descriptions are given in a book by Captain Robert B. Ross, 1/7th (Deeside Highland) Battalion, Gordon Highlanders T.F., 153rd Brigade (Highland Division): his battalion regularly took over the front from the 5th Seaforths, who were in the 152nd Brigade (Highland Division), so his descriptions of the front line, and his experiences, would be similar to those of Mackintosh. Bewsher's *History of the Fifty-First (Highland) Division* is another major source:

> The French troops were Bretons. Their great traditions
> as fighters immediately produced a bond of sympathy
> between them and the Highlanders. The Highland dress
> and the pipes evoked great interest and admiration in

---

(22) Probate Office, York

the French soldiers and in the inhabitants of the neighbouring villages, which lost nothing from the fact that the Highland Division was the first British Division to serve in that part of the country.[23]

The Highland troops were determined to make a success of the changeover.

. . . all the officers were assembled together and addressed by the Colonel. We were going to relieve a battalion of the 44th Brigade of French Infantry, recruited from Brittany and possessed of martial traditions no less renowned than our own. All that could be done to promote the *entente cordiale* was to be encouraged. As long as we were in touch with them the bonds of sympathy were to be cemented by every possible means.[24]

Scottish officers being introduced to the French trenches before their troops arrived were surprised at the catering in the front line.

Here the cuisine was not only excellent but abundant, and the Médoc imposed a warm geniality, and we opened our hearts to one another and joked as if there were no enemy for miles.[25]

When the Bretons marched away some of the Highland Division's pipe bands accompanied them for the first few miles, which pleased the Bretons:

the manner in which they refreshed the pipers during their march clearly showed their gratitude.[26]

The Pipe Major of the 8th (Argyllshire) Battalion of the Argyll

---

(23) Page 31, *History of the 51st Highland Division*, F.W.Bewsher. Blackwood, 1921

(24) Page 111, *With the Fifty-First in France*, Ross. Hodder & Stoughton 1918

(25) Ross, ibid, page 119

(26) Bewsher, ibid, page 31

and Sutherland Highlanders, in the 152nd Brigade with the 5th
Seaforths, composed a pipe tune to commemorate the event – 'The
8th Argylls Farewell to the 116eme Regiment of the Line.'[27]

The 5th Seaforths took over reserve trenches at Authuille from
the 116th regiment. Reserve trenches were the last line of defence,
and support trenches were between them and the front line. From
their rear trenches officers were introduced in small numbers to
the front line, to familiarise them before their battalion took over:

> Our men are now in the ruined village of Authuille,
> nicely ensconsed in the beautiful valley of the Ancre.
> Down this valley flows a nice little river where the water
> is clear and pure. . . parallel to the river is a railway, now
> disused. . . the battalion is disposed of in shelters of
> wood, corrugated iron, and clay in the valley near the
> railway, and on the side of the slope, where they are
> quite sheltered, or nearly so, from shell fire through the
> steepness of the hillside. Above them are the trenches,
> looking in the distance like so many zig-zag, ugly white
> scars on the beautiful scene. . . The Boche is quite near
> – in some places only 60 or 70 yards separating the two
> lines of trenches.[28]

On August 1st 1915 the 5th Seaforths' war diary records:

> Battalion in reserve trenches. 2nd. Lt.E.A.Mackintosh and
> 2nd. Lt.D.G.Wilson joined the battalion from England.
> Work parties improved the outer defences of Authuille.[29]

Mackintosh was posted to A Company, commanded by Major
MacMillan, known to his officers as 'Faither'. Fifteen days later they
withdrew for five days rest at Buire. 'The fleas in this village are of
a particularly healthy and vigorous type.'[30] While in Buire Mackin-

---

(27) Bewsher, ibid, page 32

(28) Pages 33-34 *War Diary of the 5th Seaforth Highlanders*,
   Capt.D.Sutherland. John Lane, 1920

(29) 5th Seaforths' battalion war diary., Q.O.H.museum

(30) *War Diary of the 5th Seaforth Highlanders*, ibid, page 35

tosh wrote 'Harvest',[31] comparing the conditions in which he found himself with those experienced by the ANZACS, who were still clinging to the Gallipoli Peninsula:

> Oh, you that fought your battles
> Beneath the Southern Cross,
> The earth was kinder to you,
> You could not feel the loss,
> Nor waken every morning
> And clear before you see
> The grassy fields and meadows
> Where you would wish to be.

His nostalgia for the fields and meadows is that of a man from the south of England, not that of crofters and shepherds from the great empty spaces of Caithness and Sutherland, but his interest in the ANZACS may have been an early indicator of his later plans to emigrate.[32] His early interest in Fabianism, and the knowledge that Australia and New Zealand had legislated progressive social policies may have sparked the interest, or the poem may simply have stemmed from the ANZAC predicament at Gallipoli.

On 21st August the 5th Seaforths took over the front line from the 7th (Deeside) Battalion of the Gordon Highlanders, north east of Bécourt, overlooking Sausage Valley and the village of La Boisselle. Captain Sutherland of the 5th Seaforths provides the following description of trench conditions:

> The British and German trenches in the vicinity of La Boisselle are in some places only ten yards apart, and to speak above a whisper brings over a hand grenade from the ever watchful Boche, while the chalky ground being admirably adapted for tunneling, the digging and exploding of mines under each other's lines is the order of the day, and no one ever knows when the ground may heave and rise under one's feet, hurling all in the vicinity to destruction.[33]

---

(31) *A Highland Regiment*, ibid, page 22

(32) 'Memoir', *War, The Liberator*, ibid, page 4

(33) Page 37, *War Diary of the 5th Seaforth Highlanders*

August 7th – The usual outbursts of the *mitrailleuse* – 'the
sewing machine', as the French call it, after the tric-trac
of its action. It sprays our parapet nightly. . . 11 p.m.
Two mines of a large size have exploded somewhere on
our left. They shook our puny dug-out to its very
foundations. A very violent artillery bombardment has
commenced. In the debatable region of the mines a
thick curtain of shrapnel is falling.[34]

Mackintosh wrote 'Oxford from the Trenches'[35] at Bécourt,
during his first sustained experience of the front line. The nostalgia
referred to at the end of the chapter on his time at Oxford is
balanced by a verse which illustrates the bonds already forged with
his battalion, through his training at Bedford and Golspie, and
which were being cemented on the Somme:

Here there are great things, life and death and danger,
All I ever dreamed of in the days that used to be,
Comrades and good fellowship, the soul of an army,
But, oh, it is the little things that take the heart of me.

In 'Miserere',[36] written in the trenches at La Boisselle during
one of the battalion's tours in the autumn of 1915, he addressed
the mental conflict, fought by all soldiers, which recurs in his poetry.
He contrasts youthful confidence with the anticipation of fear:

God of battles in this hour
Give us strength to suffer pain.
Lest the spirit's chains be rent,
Lest the coward flesh go free,
Unto us our prayer is sent,
Miserere Domine.

La Boisselle is the footnote to 'The Undying Race':[37] it was
written in the same period as 'Miserere', when the battalion was in

---

(34) Ross, ibid, page 131

(35) *A Highland Regiment*, ibid, page 24

(36) *A Highland Regiment*, ibid, page 25

(37) *A Highland Regiment*, ibid, page 27

the Bécourt/La Boisselle sector. The French dead were in cemeteries behind the line, and in informal graves around the trenches, where, from time to time, they would be disinterred by shellfire, and reburied, or left exposed if burial was too dangerous.

> And from their graves the Breton host
> Stand up beside the Gael.
>
> And once again our place we keep
> Against the Saxon hordes.
>
> One speech beyond their memory
> Binds us together still,
>
> Breton and Gael stand side by side
> Against the ancient foe.

He developed the same broad theme in 'The Undying Race' as he did in *Cha Till na Maccruimein*, digging into Celtic legend and linking it with the Bretons' and Highlanders' task of defeating the Saxon invaders. Such poems are evidence of his enthusiasm for the romantic folklore and culture of the Highlands, of his belief in the immortality of souls, and the indissoluble link between the past and the present. He draws on the close relationship between the Gaelic and Breton tongues, and is inspired by their common history as Celts. Mackintosh cannot have missed the irony of the fact that the Scots and Bretons were allied to the Saxons' English descendants!

On 21st September the battalion was inspected by Lord Kitchener before it went into the front line, in front of Aveluy, where the trenches were on the edge of a wood that had only been lightly damaged by shelling. All tours of duty included store carrying and trench digging in all kinds of weather. There is no evidence that Mackintosh was involved in the following episode but 'Faither' MacMillan, his company commander, emerges from the records as the kind of character who may have condoned it, and someone with Mackintosh's schoolboy sense of humour would have endorsed the expedient. Captain David Sutherland wrote:

. . . the weather was very broken with thunderstorms and heavy downpours of rain, and one company on trench digging fatigue, fertile in ideas and full of resource, before leaving their dug-outs, put off all their clothing except their boots and kilt aprons, and, thus lightly clad, they dug and shovelled for five or six hours while the rain fell in torrents. On coming off parade, this wise company hung their kilt aprons out of doors, gave themselves a good rub down, donned their nice warm underclothing and went to bed, while the other poor unfortunates had either to search for dry underclothes or shiver in their wet garments.[38]

There is a misleading lightness in this description, for Bewsher states:

The whole Division was taxed to its utmost to keep the trenches in a condition which rendered them passable to troops. This was particularly difficult in the sector between La Boisselle and Thiepval. . . the sides of the trenches fell in, and they became shapeless ditches knee or waist deep in water. . . the mud adhered to the face of the shovel and could not be flung clear of the trench. . . the frost came. . . The sides of the trenches stood as though they had been carved out of wood. For the first time for many days they went dry shod, and began to forget the unpleasant feeling of a mud-sodden kilt chafing the back of the knees, and the muddy water oozing between the toes at every step. . . this only accentuated the miseries of the inevitable thaw.[39]

Captain Ross of the 7th Gordons described Sector F.1, from north of La Boisselle to Authuille Wood, occupied by the 5th Seaforths in December 1915:

The trenches have been weathered to such an extent, both by exposure to the elemental infelicities and by

(38) Sutherland, ibid, page 40
(39) Bewsher, ibid, pages 40-41

> their subjection to hostile shelling, that it was almost a
> superhuman effort to patrol in one day the whole extent
> of the line. It was impossible, for instance, to combine
> the duties of examining the battalion bomb-stores and
> attend to the normal business of the platoon. These,
> indeed, were the particular tasks entrusted to my care,
> but I was fortunate in possessing a bombing sergeant
> whose competence was always above reproach.[40]

Like Captain Ross, Mackintosh had been appointed battalion
bombing officer – the hand grenade expert: trench warfare had
brought the revival of grenades, for clearing sections of trench. As
the bombing officer he led raids at night into No Man's Land, to
eliminate German patrols, or listening posts, where two or three
Germans would be stationed in a hole in the ground outside their
barbed wire to listen for British patrols.

Mackintosh's bad eyesight makes the decision to appoint him
bombing officer seem strange – but traditionalists were not
interested in new-fangled weapons, and an unestablished replacement officer was always likely to draw the short straw.

The August to December period was crucial to him as a young
officer, adapting the theories he had learned at Golspie and Fort
George, and relating to his brother officers and his men: he seems
to have had little trouble in this respect, and enjoyed the hours in
billets and dug-outs smoking, drinking and socialising. His
nickname was 'Tosh' or 'Toshie'.

His popularity was not limited to his own battalion: the
Highland Division was a close-knit organisation. Captain Ross, of
the 7th Gordons records:

> Time after time we relieved the 5th Seaforths, and our
> officers did not want anything better than to assemble in
> Faither's dug-out in Paisley Avenue, where, with a few
> kindred souls, such as David (Captain David Sutherland
> MC and bar: author of the *War Diary of the 5th Seaforths*)
> and Tosh and Stalker, we met the grim facts of war with
> a kind of light hearted dalliance.[41]

---

(40) Ross, ibid, page 168

(41) Ross, ibid, page 158

Although the war helped to break down social barriers, the army maintained a clear gulf between officers and the other ranks. Nonetheless, Mackintosh was as 'friendly as possible as it was for an officer to be with an N.C.O.'[42] When Mackintosh joined the battalion the writer of this reminiscence, Mr. Sinclair, was a corporal in A Company, who left for officer cadet training at the end of 1915. The fact that he was officer material may have had something to do with Mackintosh's friendship, but it does not explain his later deeply felt poems inspired by individuals who were not officers. There was a homely atmosphere in the Highland Division, derived from its peacetime recruitment from small localities throughout Scotland, which made the army's barriers between officers and men seem artificial. Regular staff officers remarked on and could not understand the friendly relationships in the Highland Division when it arrived in France.

As well as being a competent bombing officer he carved a reputation for himself at battalion concerts. Practically all entertainment near the front was homespun: in most units 'a free and easy could always be got up by having a singing competition – 1st prize, 10 fr.; 2nd. prize, 7 fr.; 3rd prize, 3fr. – with a bench of referees (against whose decision there was no appeal) sitting critically on the stage. . . and stimulating the unfortunate performers by free, caustic and personal comments when required.'[43]

In the lengthening autumn evenings, when the battalion was billeted in Hénencourt, it held concerts in the large hall at the château, and Captain David Sutherland wrote:

> Lieutenant Mackintosh cheered us with his own songs, such as 'The Smoke Helmet', 'The A.S.C.' (Army Service Corps) and 'Four and Twenty Bombers', etc, while Sgt. Mackay gave us a real Harry Lauder touch with 'Hey Donald', 'The Lass of Tobermory', and 'When the Wedding Bells are Ringing.'[44]

Sing-songs were straight out of the music hall tradition that

(42) Letter to John MacLennan from Mr. Sinclair
(43) Page 73, *A Medico's Luck in the Great War* Lt.Col D.Rorie, Milne & Hutchison, Aberdeen 1929
(44) Sutherland, ibid, page 44

Mackintosh had supported in debate in school. 'Cheered us with his own songs' suggests that he sang solo, or at least led the choruses, which would give him a more populist image amongst the men than those officers who would not join in. 'Four and Twenty Bombers'[45] was sung to the tune of 'The Ball of Kirriemuir' described accurately by Mackintosh in *War, The Liberator* as 'an ancient and disreputable Scotch ballad.' Four and twenty bombers would not often have been engaged in a bombing raid: the figure corresponds to the number of maidens in the original rendition of the Ball of Kirriemuir: 'Oh, four and twenty bombers, Ga'ed oot at La Boisselle, An' only ane cam back again, Remarkin' it was hell'.

The Army Service Corps, the A.S.C., brought forward the supplies and operated behind and up to the rear of the battlefield, and were both the envy and the butt of the front line combatants. The parody was sung to the tune of 'A Minstrel Boy to the War has Gone':[46]

The A.S.C. were driving by
When a German shell came over.
At once, determined not to die,
They one and all took cover.
Their letters home made much of the shell,
And the guns that the Huns turned on them,
They did not mention the pip-squeak fell
At least a mile beyon' them.

The schoolboy music hall entertainment was foil to the realities: at Thiepval, recalling Homer's *Odyssey*, and its hero's tribulations, Mackintosh wrote τέτλαθι δὴ κραδίη (Endure my heart):[47]

If the heart and kernel of life is rotten
What is the husk to trouble you?
Stand up straight to your work, be strong lad,
You that have lived in hell for long, lad,
Needn't be fearing to die in hell.

---

(45) *War, The Liberator*, ibid, page 112

(46) *War, The Liberator*, ibid, page 116

(47) *A Highland Regiment*, ibid, page 33

The 5th Seaforths' war diary for 29th October, 1915 states:

a bombing party went out from Hammerhead to
German listening post but found it unoccupied.[48]

This is the only reference in the war diary to patrolling, from August to Christmas 1915. 'Hammerhead' was a sap, a trench zigzagging forward from the front line through the barbed wire into No Man's Land to give protection to outgoing and incoming patrols: the saphead lay less than 200 yards from the German lines, which ran through the grounds of Thiepval Château.

Listening posts were composed of small groups of men stationed in No Man's Land as an early warning system against surprise attacks, or simply observing enemy activity, to report on it, or even to pre-empt it. Mackintosh's mission would be to deny the Germans their listening post, by attacking it with grenades and making it untenable. The troops involved would camouflage their faces with burnt cork or mud, empty their pockets of anything that would identify them if they fell into enemy hands, and remove or wrap noisy bits of equipment. They would be armed with Mills hand grenades, rifles and bayonets, some having coshes wrapped in barbed wire for close combat. Officers would have service revolvers.

The patrol would crawl out over the sandbags, make its way through prepared gaps in the British wire, and proceed with stealth towards its objective. Apart from the risks posed by alert Germans, there was danger of straying on the way back, and being mistaken for a German by a British sentry and shot. Despite efforts to ensure that adjacent friendly battalions were aware of the patrols, there were accidents. The other risk was being caught in the light of a flare, put up if a sentry suspected movement. Troops were trained to stand stock still when flares ignited.

Mackintosh captures the tensions of patrolling in 'In No Man's Land':[49] the soldiers' nervousness in the darkness is heightened by repeated references to nerve-wracking night noises, which might conceal sounds of enemy movement:

(48) 5th Seaforths' battalion war diary. Q.O.H. museum, Fort George, Inverness

(49) *A Highland Regiment*, ibid, page 29

The hedge on the left, and the trench on the right. . .

Is it the wind in the branches sighing,
Or a German trying to stop a sneeze. . .

Oh, damn you, get back to your trench, you blighter,
I really can't shoot a man with a cold.

There is caution, common sense, and awareness of the enemy's predicament in the poem. He does not give the impression of hating the Germans as individuals, and realises the common humanity of those on either side of No Man's Land. That theme is matched by another poem writtem in the Bois d'Authuille, in the early winter of 1915. 'Snow in France'[50] describes Scottish and Saxon sentries watching across the wasteland that separated them, its horrors blanketed by snow, and touches on the same theme as 'In the glen when I was young.'

We look and see the crumpled drifts
Piled in a little glen,
And you are back in Saxony
And children once again. . .

But for a little space of peace
We watch them come and go,
The children that were you and I
At play among the snow.

The battalion came out of the line on 23rd December 1915, relieved by the 16th (Boy's Brigade) Battalion, Highland Light Infantry and the 17th (Glasgow Chamber of Commerce) Battalion, Highland Light Infantry, of the 32nd Division, Kitchener volunteers. As Hogmanay (New Year's Eve) was then the principal Scottish festival, Christmas Day 1915 was a normal working day: the 5th Seaforths were in billets in Bouzincourt: A Company went to the baths, B was inspected by the Commanding Officer and C and D route marched, which was the recipe for restoring men to fitness after time in the trenches.[51]

---

(50) *A Highland Regiment*, ibid, page 31

Horse riding was a necessary accomplishment for officers in the pre-1914 army and large numbers of war-time officers had never practised the art. Colonel Davidson, the C.O., decided that all the officers should ride from Bouzincourt to Hénencourt. Mackintosh's description of the occasion was first published in the *John O' Groat Journal* on 21st January, 1916:[52]

> Sergeant Mackenzie, lengthening the stirrups until they almost touched the ground, wedged my feet, which are popularly supposed to be the largest in France today, into the smallest stirrups I have ever seen. I found myself painfully engaged in what I believe is called a canter . . . my horse rushed up alongside the Colonel, bumping me in a most unpleasant manner. The Colonel said, 'You're a junior officer; what are you doing here?' I replied, 'I'm not here on my own free will; you'll have to talk to the horse, sir! . . . and the next thing I knew I was away. . . past the football field. Every 'Fifth' man on the field immediately stopped his game, lined up and gave me a tremendous cheer as I rushed past. . . Stalk (2nd Lieutenant Robert Stalker) passed at this moment, and seeing the streak of foam from the horse on my face, shouted, 'For goodness' sake, stop him, Major, he's foaming at the mouth.'At this point Stalk's horse bolted too, and we had a hammer and tongs race up the hill, missing a mess cart coming in the opposite direction by a fraction of an inch.

Two passing Royal Engineer sappers stopped the runaway horse.

> . . . quite an assemblage turned up, including the Colonel, who was nearly falling off his horse with laughter. I departed leading the horse, which appeared to be unable to look at me without laughing. After dragging the beast along shamefacedly for a couple of

---

(51) 5th Seaforths' battalion war diary. Q.O.H. museum, Fort George, Inverness

(52) *John O'Groat Journal* 21 January 1916 and also included in Sutherland, ibid, page 51

miles I met a groom, also laughing, who took charge of
her. Now, when I meet that horse on a route march I
cannot look her in the face. Give me a quiet, self-
respecting bomb, no more horses for me!

There is a self-deprecating air to the description, and Mackintosh appears happy to have been the centre of attraction despite
his obvious incompetence with horses. That he wrote humorous
prose mirrors his willingness to pen poetic parodies, and proves
that he did not always take himself seriously.

On 29th December the battalion arrived at Molliens-au-Bois,
where it remained until 29th January 1916. There it celebrated
Hogmanay:

> . . . all the officers of the battalion, on the Colonel's
> invitation, were present at a dinner at headquarters,
> which in the present instance is part of the village school
> . . . a most interesting programme of songs and
> recitations was taken part in and, when midnight came,
> there were the usual New Year's greetings and the fervent
> hope expressed that New Year's Day 1917, would be
> ushered in in the dear homeland. . . On the return of the
> pipe band to headquarters at 12.30 a.m. after their march
> round the village, a crowd of two or three hundred men
> of the battalion followed them and the Colonel went out
> and wished them a happy New Year.[53]

Next morning the officers of the 5th Seaforths lost 2–1 to the
officers' soccer team of the 6th Seaforths, although the 5th 'had
decidedly the best of the game.'[54] In the afternoon the men of the
5th lost by the same margin to the men of the 6th.

The battalion trained for a month, route marching, taking part
in squad drill, practising attack and defence, bombing, signalling
and machine gunning. Classrooms were in barns in the village.
The Division had set up a grenade school, through which 13 officers
and 230 men were passed every week. A divisional school for infantry
was established at Villers Bocage, which ran fourteen-day courses

(53) Sutherland, ibid, page 56
(54) Sutherland, ibid, page 57

for 20 officers and 40 N.C.O.s.[55] According to the battalion war diary, 'Lt. Mackintosh rejoined from base'[56] on January 15th, but whether he had been on a grenade course, at the infantry school, or coming back from leave, is not recorded. Mackintosh had his photograph taken at Molliens-au-Bois or nearby, dressed in the sheepskin waistcoat issued to the troops: the bloom of youth of his original commissioning photograph has disappeared and he looks weary.

From 29th January until the 4th of February the troops were at Acheux, making a railway. There was a metre gauge line from Doullens to Albert. Acheux was roughly halfway along the line, and it had been decided to construct a single line standard gauge branch from Candas, on the main Arras to Amiens line, to Acheux. Although each division had a labour battalion, dedicated to navvying and trench digging, the manpower of all the battalions had to be utilised to undertake the labouring necessary to support the war. Between 8th and 20th February the battalion was at Corbie: 'where for twelve days the battalion had a delightful change of scene from the smelly farming villages and dirty barns and outhouses which have been their rest billets since coming to France.'[57]

Appreciating that these were the good times, when the battalion was out of the line, and that there would be an offensive in the future, with death as its inevitable accompaniment, Mackintosh wrote 'Before the Summer' at Corbie:[58]

When our men are marching lightly up and down,
When the pipes are playing in the little town,
I see a thin line swaying through wind and mud and rain
And the broken regiments come back to rest again.

Lest we see a worse thing than it is to die,
Live ourselves and see our friends cold beneath the sky,
God grant we too be lying there in wind and mud and rain
Before the broken regiments come stumbling back again.

---

(55) Bewsher, ibid, Chapter IV

(56) 5th Seaforths' battalion war diary. Q.O.H. museum, Fort George, Inverness

(57) Sutherland, ibid, page 58

(58) *A Highland Regiment,* ibid, page 37

It is a prescient piece, burdened with the thought of unbearable grief, with death the only alternative to it: it might be taken as a death wish. Or it may be evidence that he has seen the horrors of war, lost friends, felt the grief of empty places in the mess, and the loss of comradeship that represented, and is beginning to feel anticipatory guilt at the thought that he might survive when others fell: this could be an early sign of post-traumatic stress syndrome, of which survivor's guilt is a recognised sign.

On 20th February the battalion went to live in tents in the Bois des Tailles while they repaired roads reduced to gravelly slush by lack of maintenance, heavy traffic, snow and frost. A German plane bombed them while they were playing football, but did no damage. It left Corbie on the 28th and after a week at Molliens-au-Bois moved via Beauval and Ivergny to Louiez, to relieve French troops at the south end of Vimy Ridge.[59]

Two months of training, railway construction and roadmaking were at an end. 'Before the Summer' is the only poem from this period of rest: the next poems are prompted by a major event in his personal and military experience. The irregularity of his output of poems indicates that he wrote when he had something specific to say, or that he was not a poseur, versifying for appearances sake – or, if he did versify, he destroyed the results.

The months on the Somme had been Mackintosh's introduction to war: the next few months would take him to the peak of his military efficiency, and the intensity of his experience was to inspire some of his most powerful poems.

---

(59) 5th Seaforths' battalion war diary. Q.O.H. museum, Fort George, Inverness

TO MY SISTER

If I die tomorrow
I shall go happily.
With the flush of battle on my face
I shall walk with an eager pace
The road I cannot see.

My life burnt fiercely always,
And fiercely will go out
With glad wild fighting ringed around,
But you will be above the ground
And darkness all about.

You will not hear the shouting,
You will not see the pride,
Only with tortured memory
Remember what I used to be,
And dream of how I died.

You will see gloom and horror
But never the joy of fight,
You'll dream of me in pain and fear,
And in your dreaming never hear
My voice across the night.

My voice that sounds so gaily
Will be too far away
For you to see across your dream
The charging and the bayonet's gleam,
Or hear the words I say.

And parted by the warders
That hold the gates of sleep,
I shall be dead and happy
And you will live and weep.

The Labyrinth, May 15, 1916
A Highland Regiment

THE CHARGE OF THE LIGHT BRIGADE
(Brought up to date)

Half a league, half a league,
Half a league onward –
'That is, unless some damned
Airman has blundered,
If the map isn't right
We'll be a funny sight.'
So as they tramped along
Officers pondered,
While, with equipment hung,
Curses on every tongue,
Forward with rifles slung,
Slouched the six hundred.

Cannon to right of them,
Cannon to left of them,
Cannon in front of them
Volleyed and thundered,
'And-what was twice as bad –
Our gunners never had
Strafed that machine-gun lad.
I always wondered
If our old barrage could
Be half as bloody good
As the Staff said it would.'
Was there a man dismayed?
Yes, they were damned afraid,
Loathing both shot and shell,
Into the mouth of Hell,
Sticking it pretty well,
Slouched the six hundred.

Through the barrage they passed,
Men falling thick and fast,
Till the machine-gun blast
Smote them to lying
Down in the grass a bit;
Over the roar of it
Officers yelled, were hit,
Dropped and lay dying.
Then the retreat began,
Every unwounded man
Staggered or crawled or ran
Back to the trench again,
While on the broken plain
Dead and untroubling,
Wounded and wondering,
What help the night would bring,
Lay the six hundred.

War, The Liberator

IN MEMORIAM
PRIVATE D. SUTHERLAND,
KILLED IN ACTION IN THE GERMAN TRENCH, MAY 1916,
AND THE OTHERS WHO DIED

So you were David's father,
And he was your only son,
And the new-cut peats are rotting
And the work is left undone,
Because of an old man weeping,
Just an old man in pain,
For David, his son David,
That will not come again.

Oh, the letters that he wrote you,
And I can see them still,
Not a word of the fighting
But just the sheep on the hill
And how you should get the crops in
Ere the year got stormier,
And the Bosches have got his body,
And I was his officer.

You were only David's father,
But I had fifty sons
When we went up in the evening
Under the arch of the guns,
And we came back at twilight –
O God! I heard them call
To me for help and pity
That could not help at all.

Oh, never will I forget you,
My men that trusted me,
More my sons than your fathers',
For they could only see
The little helpless babies
And the young men in their pride.
They could not see you dying,
And hold you while you died.

Happy and young and gallant,
They saw their first-born go,
But not the strong limbs broken
And the beautiful men brought low,
The piteous writhing bodies,
The screamed, 'Don't leave me, Sir,'
For they were only your fathers
But I was your officer.

A Highland Regiment

Rosemary Beazley

Alan Mackintosh at Molliens au Bois, 1916
in winter issue clothing

CHAPTER 4
THE LABYRINTH

'Tosh and his squad of bombers are very busy these
nights for there are almost nightly patrol encounters in
no-man's-land, or in attacks on the saps which here
extend some distance forward of the front line.'

D. Sutherland,
War Diary of the 5th Seaforth Highlanders

When the 51st (Highland) Division took over a new sector
between Roclincourt and Neuville St. Vaast, north of
Arras, in March 1916, its soldiers needed to display in
abundance the bombing, sniping and trench warfare skills learned
in the Somme. These skills had been updated and much improved
by the divisional schools held during their time out of the line.
Though such activities were hindered somewhat by spells of bad
weather, Bewsher recalled that the Division: '. . . after its six week
period of rest and training, was at the top of its form, and presented
a most soldierly appearance.'[1]

The new sector had previously been held by the French. During
their tenure the fighting had been so stubborn that the French and
Germans had dug themselves in very close to each other time after
time, resulting in a complex maze of trenches known as 'The
Labyrinth'. The loss of life had been severe, and Captain Sutherland
notes that the Highland troops continually came across evidence
of this as they settled in:

A new trench cannot be dug without coming on the
hastily buried dead, grisly hands stick out of the present
trenches, while one machine gun crew, in making a

---

(1) Page 55, *History of the Fifty-First Highland Division 1914-1918*,
F.W. Bewsher. Blackwood, 1921

recess for their gun, tried four times before they found a spot clear of bodies.[2]

General Harper, who commanded the 51st (Highland) Division, took over command of the sector on 12th March, 1916, making his headquarters at Duisans, while various elements of the Division were based in villages behind the line, which was overlooked by Vimy Ridge and Observatory Ridge.

An informal account by Captains Peel and Macdonald of the 6th Seaforths describes the position:

> At our backs were the villages of Anzin and Maroeuil, while the trenches themselves were in a hollow plateau, the ground sloping upward again on the enemy's side, forming the well-known Vimy Ridge on our left, and showing the tops of the villages of Farbus and Thélus on our immediate front. On our right again the ground sloped downwards towards the ruins of Roclincourt.[3]

The 5th Seaforths were in the village of Maroeuil, before moving into the front line trenches nearby on 11th March. The Division finished its relief of the French by the 14th, despite a severe blizzard:

> During this period the troops could do no more than remain where they had been placed by their guides, or misplaced, as the case might be. During the relief and until the blizzard abated, officers and men had only a hazy idea as to where they actually were.[4]

This relative inactivity did not last long. When the weather cleared there were frequent attacks to carry out or repulse, very often fighting in or between the craters left by the explosion of mines, or in the saps that were dug to connect craters to the front line:

---

(2) Page 61, *War Diary of the 5th Seaforth Highlanders*, Capt D.Sutherland. John Lane, 1920

(3) *The Great War, 1914-1918. 6th Seaforth Highlanders, Campaign Reminiscences,*. Capt. R.T.Peel MC and Capt. A.H. Macdonald MC W.R. Walker and Co., Elgin, 1923

(4) Bewsher, ibid, page 57

In these encounters casualties were frequently heavy, as
the parties often had to pass through a heavy barrage,
followed by their bomb carriers. The latter were employed
in large numbers, as in this form of warfare several
hundred bombs were often thrown in one night.[5]

Among others similarly employed, Mackintosh and his bombers
were much in demand, and he was chosen to lead an important
raid on a German salient in May, a raid mentioned in Bewsher as
one of the 'two most successful taking place in this period.' In
addition to the hazards of opposing fire and counter-attack which
such raiding parties might expect to experience, the German
trenches were commonly up to ten or twelve feet deep (3-4 metres)
and lined with planks; this made entry and exit extremely difficult,
particularly if there were casualties to be evacuated at the end of
the raid. The raid was in retaliation for the detonation of a mine
and a raid on the 6th Seaforths on 28th April, which had cost the
6th Seaforths 5 officers and 62 other ranks: of that total 15 were
killed and 19 missing, probably blown apart or buried by the
explosion of the mine.[6] The enemy who made the attack were
Bavarians.[7] In addition to retaliation the raiding party was to destroy
dug-outs and take prisoners, from whom information could be
obtained. Maybe this incident was the inspiration for Mackintosh's
poem 'Mines' that he wrote in 1917.

The raid was scheduled for the evening of May 16th, and a
party of fifty men, selected from a hundred volunteers was trained
over a two week period by Mackintosh and 2nd Lt. C.E. Mackay.
Captain Ross 7th Gordon Highlanders, gives a description of typical
preparations for a later raid in the Labyrinth:

> Picked volunteers practised for the coup with zealous
> industry. The scene of their rehearsals was well behind
> the lines. The trenches to be raided were represented by
> tapes, accurately laid down and assiduously studied. All
> concerted to bring the forthcoming episode to a
> triumphal conclusion. The spirit of manly exercise was

(5) Bewsher, ibid, page 60.

(6) Peel and Macdonald, ibid, page 21

(7) Peel and Macdonald, ibid, page 20

encouraged and exceptional privileges were conceded to foster the offensive vigour . . .[8]

Mackintosh and Mackay (the two officers) carried out as much reconnaissance as they could of the ground to be covered; there were also personal preparations to make. Although Captain Sutherland did not name him in the following story in his history of the 5th Seaforths, there is little doubt that the raider with the 'poetic' mind was Mackintosh, particularly since the story concludes with a note of wry humour which is typical of him:

> One of the raiders, realising the uncertainty of human life, especially when on raiding bent, resolved to put his affairs in order before setting out, and, among other things, sent cheques to liquidate his debts, included among which was an item of 8/9d. incurred while in the north previous to coming out – a debt which, for various reasons, he had vowed never to pay, and yet he sent a cheque for it as for the others. In the hurry of the moment, and as one would expect of a mind which is more poetic than business-like, he wrote the cheque for 9/8d. instead. Having come back safely from the raid, the first regret was ever having paid the debt, and the second that he paid 11d. more than he ought.[9]

It is clear that the possibility of death was very much in Mackintosh's mind. He was going to lead his men in fading daylight, as distinct from crawling about in No Man's Land in the dark. The raid was designed to be unsubtle, aggressive, destructive and vengeful and bore no resemblance to listening post duty in No Man's Land, or even night trench raids, where the crossing of No Man's Land was made as unobtrusively as possible, before the last few moments of the assault. This was to be as close to conventional 'going over the top' as Mackintosh had experienced, and all the responsibility lay on his shoulders. The chances of being hit were greater than operating in the dark and any hesitation that could be

---

(8) Page 188, *The Fifty First in France*, Capt.R.B.Ross. Hodder and Stoughton, 1918

(9) Sutherland, D., ibid, page 68

construed as cowardice would be more obvious to his men in daylight. The battalion would be depending on him, and the brigadier. It was a 'show', however small, in which he was the principal player.

Mackintosh was an aesthete, not an unimaginative philistine; a poet by nature, not a warrior. Fear of showing fear would have seized him, as would fear itself. He would have gone through all the possibilities in his mind, and tried to dismiss them one by one, but fear would remain – of pain, of dying, of showing fear, of making the wrong decision, of letting down his men, his battalion and himself. He would have suffered all the stomach-churning anxieties of any normal person faced with the prospect of attacking over an exposed stretch of blasted earth.

He would have countered his terror by calling on his courage and will to win: a concoction of learned tradition, personal pride, *esprit de corps*, loyalty to his men, religion and patriotism. In modern parlance, he would have wound himself up emotionally to do the job in hand. This is clear from his poem 'To My Sister'[10] which is dated May 15th, the day before the raid:

If I die tomorrow
I shall go happily
With the flush of battle on my face
I shall walk with an eager pace
The road I cannot see.

My life burnt fiercely always,
And fiercely will go out
With glad fighting ringed around. . .

It would be wrong to dismiss this poem as one of the overly romantic genre written by poets before they have been in action: though not as yet involved in a major action Mackintosh had already seen enough of the tragedy and torment of war, and had articulated his thoughts on them in earlier poems, for such an assessment to be untenable. It is more likely that at a time of great stress and apprehension, he naturally reverts to simpler ways of expressing himself. In addition he is bridging the gulf which necessarily exists

(10) Page 38, E.A.Mackintosh, *A Highland Regiment* John Lane, The Bodley Head, 1917

between himself, a combatant, and his sister at home, who will, however, recognise the truth of such personally descriptive lines as: 'My life burnt fiercely always. . .'

This contrasts with the dispirited tone of many of his pre-war post-romance poems, and indicates that he had found purpose in his life. The sister to whom this poem was addressed was probably Muriel, who had been given charge of his poetic works in his will.

On the day of the raid the rest of the battalion was in reserve and engaged in working parties. Mackintosh gave a very full account of the events of that day in the prose account 'A Raid'[11] (published in *War, The Liberator* as one of three 'studies in war psychology'). The names of the participants were changed in various ways, though the consequent disguise of names is no more than superficial in several cases. He may have disguised the names for security reasons, or because it was then unfashionable to write in the first person about acts of personal heroism. The raiders have been dismissed from parade after being instructed to assemble at 2.15 p.m. in full raiding equipment. Mackintosh, who has called himself MacTaggart and Mackay ('Macrae') watch them go:[12]

> The fifty big men turned to their right, slapped their rifles and broke off in twos and threes towards their billet. As they went in, one splendid looking boy of nineteen or twenty seized a friend by the waist and brought him down after a short struggle.
> 'You look out, De Wet,' said his sergeant, an English Highlander, 'or you'll be too tired to get at the Germans.' The boy looked up, flashing a smile at him. 'Tired? I'll not get tired,' he said, 'this is chust my trainin',' and followed the rest into the billet.

'De Wet' and the 'English Highlander' are both important participants in later events. It is interesting that Mackintosh uses the term 'English Highlander': this description is just as applicable to Mackintosh himself, although he would believe that his family background made him a Scot. He recounts a whole range of

---

(11) Pages 121-142, E.A.Mackintosh, *War, The Liberator* John Lane, The Bodley Head, 1918

(12) *War, The Liberator*, ibid, page 121

attitudes, thoughts and fears during the hours before the raid. Watching the men at the parade he is buoyantly (and by modern standards almost repellently) optimistic:[13]

> 'My God, Charles,' said the Senior Subaltern
> (Mackintosh/MacTaggart), 'aren't they great? God help
> any Bosche that meets those lads. They're just as fit and
> happy as they can be. I feel top-hole too, don't you? I
> don't see that there's anything that can spoil it.'

His fellow officer sounds a note of caution about the German barbed wire, bringing Mackintosh down to earth. He retorts fatalistically:[14]

> 'Oh, damn the wire, . . . if there's any bombardment at
> all, it'll go west; and there's going to be a hell of a
> bombardment. Anyhow, we can't do any more.'

During lunch Mackintosh deals with his fear by portraying in tongue-in-cheek fashion the painful scene that would take place if he were brought back dead from the raid, all the while feeling that the forthcoming event is almost unreal and like a game of 'let us pretend'. At 2.15 p.m. pontoon wagons loaned by the Royal Engineers arrive to transport the raiding party. On the way up the line talk gradually ceases, until by the time they are walking up the communication trench, the only sound is the heavy breathing of one of the sergeants:[15]

> 'I'm sorry hurrying you, Sergeant Dunnet,' said the
> Senior Subaltern, 'but we've got to be at battalion
> Headquarters at 5, although I don't suppose zero'll be
> for a good time after that.'

Mackintosh is anxious to arrive at Battalion Headquarters well before the start time, which would only be made known to him there. It is not clear who Sergeant Dunnet actually was, though a

---

(13) *War, The Liberator*, ibid, page 121

(14) *War, The Liberator*, ibid, page 122

(15) *War, The Liberator*, ibid, page 124

connection with Dunnet, near Thurso, is unlikely. However, there is here a rather apt word play on two names, since the young Private De Wet mentioned earlier quite conceivably becomes 'Do It' whilst 'Dunnet' completes a comment on the two men's ages and differing physical conditions. This touch of Mackintosh humour indicates the regard he had for his men, and also underlines the fact that both the young and not-so-young were to risk their lives in the raid.

As the party passes officers and men of the 5th Seaforths in the reserve trench near Brigade Headquarters Mackintosh receives an invitation to tea with officer friends in A Company. The battalion C.O., Colonel A.H. Spooner, tells him that the bombardment will not start until 8 p.m., and that the men call fall out until 7 p.m. The following extract from their conversation demonstrates Mackintosh's ability for self-observation in his writing, the attention given to near domestic detail being a defence against fear and impending danger:[16]

> 'Seven will do,' said the C.O., 'but what have you done
> to yourself? I've never seen you looking so smart. Is that
> a new tunic?'
> 'Well, sir,' said Mactaggart with a grin, 'I thought I
> might as well get killed like a gentleman.'
> 'You are a gruesome young devil,' said the Adjutant. 'Are
> you coming to tea at Headquarters?'
> 'Well, as a matter of fact we've got a previous invitation
> coupled with a salmon from A Coy,' replied the graceless
> youth, 'and unless you've got anything better. . .'

Also present at the meal in the dug-out was Captain David Sutherland (author of the battalion history) who lent Mackintosh his watch to take with him on the raid. After tea Mackintosh and Mackay take their leave: a certain calmness, and feelings of unreality about the approaching attack, have replaced their earlier fear. At Headquarters the assembled party is addressed by Brigadier-General W.C. Ross, who commanded the 152nd Brigade until July 1916 and was himself 'a Highlander and veteran of three wars', thus being much respected by those present:[17]

---

(16) *War, The Liberator*, ibid, page 126

'You're going to help make the name of the regiment,
and the fame of the North, tonight, men. I've heard that
in Flanders yesterday the Bosche came up against
Scotsmen again and got the worst of it. Now you'll show
'em today that Scotland can give them the worst of it
here, too. Scotland for ever. Lead on, Mr. MacTaggart,
and good luck,' and the raiding party filed up the long
communication trench to the front line.

The evening is still extraordinarily quiet, with only the sound
of a plane overhead; Mackintosh is now quite fearful of how he will
perform when the time comes, but is moved by the good wishes of
his Highland comrades, who evidently hold him in esteem:[18]

'Good luck, sir. Good luck, boys!' N.C.O.s and men of
their battalion stood to attention as they passed up, and a
lump came into the Senior Subaltern's throat. Suppose he
had lost his nerve. . . Savagely he fought his doubts,
reminding himself of past risks lightly taken, heartening
himself with the phrase he had heard the men use, 'they
cannae kill our officer,' and partially succeeded. But the
abysmal doubt persisted somewhere in his brain, as it had
done always before action, and probably always would.

At the support trench Mackintosh and Mackay take half each
of the party and move to the two starting-off points established in
craters. Mackintosh's men enter theirs through a preceding trench
and crater. His concern about being on time is unnecessary, since
they are several minutes early:[19]

The men composed themselves to wait in easy attitudes,
but each one had a nervous trick betraying his tense
condition. Some licked their dry lips again and again,
some felt their bayonets. One red-haired fellow took out all
his bombs, one by one, and squeezed their pins pensively.

(17) *War, The Liberator*, ibid, page 127

(18) *War, The Liberator*, ibid, page 128

(19) *War, The Liberator*, ibid, page 130

The artillery preparation had now started. This took the form of a box barrage, which isolates the section of line to be attacked and aims to prevent reinforcements to it by the enemy. In time for the attack the central part of the bombardment moves deeper into the enemy defences to allow the raiders the opportunity to advance into the enemy trench. There is a problem in respect of descriptions of Mackintosh's raid, in that the available accounts vary the period, timing and nature of the bombardment.

Captain Sutherland[20] has the bombardment starting in great force just before 8 p.m. and the advance after twenty minutes or so, therefore about 8.15 p.m., although he was by now minus his own watch, loaned to Mackintosh.[21]

In 'A Raid' Mackintosh mentions being told that the time for the bombardment was to be X.20 (8.20 p.m.)[22] with the advance at 8.25 p.m., still with a difference of several minutes even if Captain Sutherland's account is inaccurate. In 'A Raid' what is happening at 'X' seems to have been the general evening bombardment,[23] usually involving trench mortars, not the fierce beginning of the 'show' (Sutherland)[24] in particular, which accords with the nature of the bombardment related by Mackintosh as taking place on time only a few minutes before the advance. Furthermore, the official battalion records say that the advance began at 8.10 p.m. after the bombardment.[25]

Since all the writers were close to the event in terms of time and place, there seems to be no conclusive reason as to why such variations exist, thus raising questions as to whether there may have been some actual mistiming or confusion. Captain Sutherland vividly describes the nature of the barrage:[26]

> . . . our artillery began the show by raining a hail of
> shells supplemented by trench mortars, directed on each

(20) Sutherland, ibid, page 66

(21) *War, The Liberator*, ibid, page 126

(22) *War, The Liberator*, ibid, page 124

(23) *War, The Liberator*, ibid, page 130

(24) Sutherland, ibid, page 66

(25) 5th Seaforths' battalion war diary. Q. O. H. museum, Fort George, Inverness

(26) Sutherland, ibid, page 66

side and behind the area to be raided. To these the
Bosche vigorously replied, and in a minute or two the
place was a screaming inferno of shells and bombs, our
front line heavily swept by their fire. It is computed that
in three-quarters of an hour our artillery fired 2000
shells on this small sector of the front, so one can
picture the din. It was now dusk, and the flashes of the
guns, the flame of bursting shrapnel, the pale light of
star-shells, transformed what was a beautifully calm
moonlit night into a whirlwind of devastation and death.

As he counts down to zero, Mackintosh laughs to himself as he
remembers, incongruously, the cox counting down to the starting
gun in his boating days at Oxford. Then, at last, the time comes:[27]

'Half a minute more,' he passed along, and watched the
seconds ticking past. Then all at once he climbed up,
and, for a second or two, stood alone on the crater lip.
'Come along, boys,' he said quietly, and the raiding
party poured after him across into the open.

Mackintosh discards his wire-cutters on finding that the shelling
has opened a way through the wire in front of the German trench.
Now his mood is one of strange exultation, and he is almost
disappointed on climbing down into the deep German trench to have
found everything quiet at first. Then the unreality dissipates:[28]

'It's a dug-out,' said a man's voice from very far away,
and suddenly he was aware of bullets hitting the side of
the trench, and four Bosches stumbling up the dug-out
steps, and shouting as they came. All at once his brain
began to act rapidly.

Mackintosh pulls a bomb from his haversack, and throws it at
the approaching Germans, leaping sideways to avoid the blast.
Three fall, while the fourth leans against the side of the trench with
his hands to his face:[29]

---

(27) *War, The Liberator*, ibid, page 131
(28) *War, The Liberator*, ibid, page 132

> A savage joy possessed the Senior Subaltern, and he
> shoved the revolver close to the man's face and fired.
> Those clutching hands dropped, and the German crashed
> to the steps with the back of his head blown away.

Mackintosh rushes along the trench to meet Mackay's party at the point of the salient, nearly mistaking them for Germans until he notices their kilts. Here horror and humour are continued as he turns to bomb the large dug-out at the point of apex of the salient:[30]

> From below there came a shout, 'You bastards! You
> English bastards. 'English be _____!' yelled a man
> behind him hoarsely, 'Scotch, you _____ liars,' and a
> bomb shot down the stair. Even in the midst of the
> shouting and explosions, he had time to laugh at that.

One of his men now approaches from the right, Mackintosh seeing 'one of the most terrible sights in the world, fear in the eyes of a brave man.'[31] The wounded soldier is followed by another, who screams that he has been wounded 'by our own _____ shells.'

Now a whole group of men in a similar state come along, and Mackintosh gives the general signal to retire. Is Mackintosh suggesting that the barrage is falling at the wrong place at that point? If so, then perhaps one of the hidden reasons for writing the account was to indicate the possibility of tragic mistakes having been made, without attempting to apportion blame.

Mackintosh is about to leave the trench when his English sergeant, Godstone, alerts him to the fact that three severely wounded men still remain some way along the trench. Mackintosh is honest enough to admit his temporary doubt about going back to rescue them:[32]

> Then he remembered a score of things – his promise
> that he wouldn't go back and leave one of them alive in
> the German trench, his pride that his men had always

(29) *War, The Liberator*, ibid, page 132
(30) *War, The Liberator*, ibid, page 133
(31) *War, The Liberator*, ibid, page 133
(32) *War, The Liberator*, ibid, page 135

trusted him and followed him, his affection for the men, and, above all, the eternal principle, as old as war, an officer can't desert his men.

Mackay watches the left of the trench-line, while Mackintosh and Sergeant Godstone return to the men, whom they find in a blood-stained bay. The first they come to is De Wet, the young man who had wrestled with his chum in the morning. Both his legs are missing below the thigh. They first drag another man up the twelve foot parapet to a shell hole, Mackintosh relating a quite unreasonable impatience with him, until the man is recognised as being Thomson, the only participant not to receive some measure of disguise in the account. Records and a process of elimination indicate that this was Private Andrew Thompson, from Belfast.[33]

Mackintosh then returns on his own to the other two, by then feeling very weak and helpless himself. One man says in an accent which is obviously Scottish: 'Ma airm an' ma leg's off.'[34] He was most probably Lance Corporal Angus Macdonald from Skye,[35] given the pseudonym MacNeil to differentiate him from 'Macdonald', Mackintosh's bombing sergeant, who now returns from the British front line to assist his officer. This is opportune, as Mackintosh is having to bomb the trench behind him in order to repel advancing Germans, who appear despite the bombardment and the clearance of the Germans' dug-outs by both halves of the raiding party. Mackintosh now feels considerably better:[36]

Suddenly he felt 'This is all right. I'm going to get through. We're all going to get through. And isn't wee Macdonald a damned fine chap to come back for me like that?'

Together they bring MacNeil to the point of the salient and up

(33) Enquiries Dept, Commonwealth War Graves Commision. Soldiers Died in the Great War Part 64 Seaforth Highlanders. reprint. J.B.Hayward and Son 1988

(34) *War, The Liberator*, ibid, page 137

(35) *Soldiers Died in the Great War* (Reprint), J.B.Hayward and Son, 1988

(36) *War, The Liberator*, ibid, page 138

and on to the parapet, going back again for the legless boy, whose condition has deteriorated. Despite his entreaties to leave him Mackintosh will not desert him:[37]

> 'Rot', said his officer, and up to the point they dragged
> him and tried to lift the dead weight to the top. All at
> once MacTaggart's strength seemed to leave him, and
> his arms were powerless to move the heavy body.

Mackay helps to lift the soldier, while Mackintosh returns to drag MacNeil into an old trench leading to their front line, then assists Godstone with Thompson. German guns are now pounding the parapet area with great ferocity. Mackintosh momentarily seems to become detached from himself and is an observer of the scene:[38]

> . . . he seemed to be regarding himself from the front
> stalls of a gigantic theatre and applauding a fine piece
> of acting. He wouldn't get through it, and nobody would
> know, but he was doing the right thing, and painting a
> good picture. The aesthetic joy of it buoyed him up. . .

He returns to where Mackay and Godstone are still struggling with the soldier:[39]

> He looked down at the shrunken face.
> 'I believe we'll have to leave him, Charles,' he said, 'he's
> a dying man.'
> Charlie MacRae looked up with his hand on the boy's
> heart.
> 'No, he isn't,' he said, 'he's dead.'

This soldier was Private Davis Sutherland from Achreamie,[40] near Dounreay, Caithness. Though Private Thompson and Lance

---

(37) *War, The Liberator*, ibid, page 138

(38) *War, The Liberator*, ibid, page 139

(39) *War, The Liberator*, ibid, page 139

(40) Commonwealth War Graves Commission. Soldiers Died in
the Great War, ibid

Corporal Macdonald died on the day after the raid,[41] and Private John McDowell of Belfast was killed on returning to the British lines by a bomb which burst in his haversack,[42] Private Sutherland was the only one to be left in the German trench, which was a source of continuing grief for Mackintosh. The remaining part of the struggle to bring back the wounded seems interminable to Mackintosh. They are still being pursued, and more than one man calls upon God, each in his own way:[43]

> One of the wounded men, a Catholic, began to confess his sins as they dragged him along. Once Sergeant Godstone prayed for strength to get them in, and MacTaggart heard himself crying, 'Oh, God, let's get these poor devils in, and I don't care what happens.'

There is a terrible moment when Mackintosh accuses a comrade of being a coward for not helping, then realises that it is Mackay, who has been wounded along with the bombing sergeant (R.N. Morrison from Kinlochbervie). They both return to help despite their wounds. Then, finally, it is over:[44]

> . . . now at the mouth of our sap were the stretcher bearers to give them a hand, and wire half-cut, easy to get through for whole men, but making the wounded scream with pain; while in the broken hole crouched MacTaggart telling the rest to get in and he would cover their retreat, till suddenly the British shrapnel cloaked the German line, and for five minutes our own machine-guns screamed over his head. Then, all at once, the tumult stopped dead, and in the stillness there came from the salient a single flare.

The time at which the British artillery targets the German trench after the raiders have left it comes arguably rather late in the retreat.

---

(41) Commonwealth War Graves Commission Soldiers Died in the Great War, ibid

(42) *John O' Groat Journal* May 26th 1916, per Ally Budge

(43) *War, The Liberator*, ibid, page 140

(44) *War, The Liberator*, ibid, page 140

However, if this had happened earlier, increased 'friendly fire' casualties could well have resulted, though the level of German retaliation would have been reduced. Once out of danger, Mackintosh is overwhelmed by grief and is given a clout on the head by his 'dear Major' to prevent him from rushing back to the German line to avenge the fate of his men. The Major was 'Faither', A.L. MacMillan. Realising that Mackintosh needs a drink, 'Faither' takes him back to the Battalion Headquarters. First Mackintosh goes to the dressing station and realises from the survivors' reports that the raid had really succeeded. Then he meets Sergeant Godstone:

> At H.Q. was Sergeant Godstone sitting on the steps with his head in his hands – it was from his section that the dead had come. The C.O. gave them both strong whiskies, and brought in Charles MacRae for another. Then they went to Brigade H.Q., to receive the thanks of the Brigadier, and lastly, jolted off, he and Godstone together, in a mess-cart back to the village again.

Sergeant Godstone was Sergeant Robert Goddard,[45] who finished the war as a Company Sergeant Major with a Military Medal and Bar. Writing of the raid he recalled:

> 2nd Lt Stalker who he (Mackintosh) refers to was one of the officers in my own company at the time of the Raid and lent me his Revolver a thing which few officers would do knowing the chances of seeing their revolver again and in pulling in an Irishman with his leg hanging the Revolver which was hanging from the lanyard got mixed up with the wire and I couldn't afford the time to untwist it under the circumstances and I slipped my shoulder through it and left it there and when it was all over I remembered that I had lost the revolver and felt

---

(45) Letter from Robert Goddard to Muriel Mackintosh. (When he wrote this he was at his father's farm at Denton, near Canterbury, recovering from major surgery to his jaw and hoping to 'resume my old emplyment of Compositor next Spring, that is if my nerves and memory is better.'

rather uncomfortable about it and told Mr Stalker I
would go out another night and recover it or buy him a
new one but he said he wouldn't hear of my doing either
and said he could easily get another Revolver but not
another Serg G.

On his return to the village, Mackintosh is angered by a piper's
rendition of 'Highland Laddie', which does not fit in with his mood.
The landlady at his billet asks about Charles Mackay:[46]

'*Mais ou est l'autre officer?*' Mackintosh replies: '*Il est
blessé, Madame. . . mais nous avons tué plus que quarante
Bosches. . . et je suis très fatigué.*' ('He is wounded,
Madame. . . but we killed more than forty Bosches. . .
and I am very tired.')

The actual number of German casualties was estimated at
between sixty and seventy, and a total of five dug-outs had been
successfully bombed.[47] British casualties were by comparison
considered slight, since there were four dead and thirteen wounded
from a total of fifty one participants, including the officers. The
Commander of XVII Corps, Lt. General J.H.G. Byng, sent the
following message of congratulation:[48]

Corps Commander desires to convey to the Officers,
N.C.O.s and men of the 5th Battalion Seaforth
Highlanders his highest appreciation of their
enterprising and successful raid on the enemy trenches
on the evening of the 16th.

The raid was given prominence in *The Times* of May 18th,[49]
which is mentioned by Mackintosh in a letter to one of his sisters;
this letter was included in *War, The Liberator* in an introduction –
curiously not appearing in all the editions – written by Coningsby

---

(46) *War, The Liberator*, ibid, page 142
(47) 5th Seaforths' battalion war diary. Q.O.H. museum, Fort
George, Inverness
(48) Sutherland, ibid, page 68
(49) *The Times*, 18th May 1916

Dawson, another Bodley Head author of that era. The letter is of considerable interest since it gives Mackintosh's earliest written reaction to the raid:[50]

> You will probably have noticed in the official report that a raid was made on the 16th on the trenches at _____. That, my dearest, was me and I don't want to do another. . . Our losses were slight, but three of my men had their legs blown off in the Bosches' trench and we had to pull them out and get them back. I and Charles M____ and Sergeant G_____ were alone, and I can tell you it was no joke pulling a helpless man a yard, and then throwing a bomb to keep the Bosches back – then pulling him another yard and throwing another bomb . . . Sergeant M and Charles got wounded, but they both came back to us again until the men were in. I just gave myself up. The shrapnel was bursting right in my face and the machine-guns – ugh! I wasn't touched except for a hole in my hose-top. I didn't stop swearing the whole time, except when I was praying – but I'd promised the men I wouldn't leave the Bosche trench while there was a man alive in it and I kept my word. . . All the men I have brought back have died.
> I believe I've been recommended for the Military Cross, but I'd rather have the boys' lives. If I get one, I'll get home on special leave soon. I've had my taste of a show. It's not romantic. It's hell.

Again, the opposition noted seems to belie the quality of the artillery support, as do references in Mackintosh's parody of the 'Charge of The Light Brigade':[51]

> And – what was twice as bad –
> Our gunners never had
> Strafed that machine-gun lad.
> I always wondered

---

(50) Introduction by Coningsby Dawson, _War, The Liberator_

(51) _War, The Liberator_, ibid, page 90

If our old barrage could
Be half as bloody good
As the Staff said it would

Through the barrage they passed
Men falling thick and fast. . .

Mackintosh was awarded the Military Cross, gazetted on 24th June:[52]

> For conspicuous gallantry. He organised and led a
> successful raid on the enemy's trenches with great skill
> and courage. Several of the enemy were disposed of and
> a strong point destroyed. He also brought back two
> wounded men under fire.
>
> (*London Gazette*, 24th June 1916)

Lance Sergeant R. Morrison, Private D. Cameron and Private G. Grant were awarded Military Medals. One of Mackintosh's most moving and oft-quoted poems, 'In Memoriam', was written about the raid. It expresses his grief for those killed, and features, in particular, Private David Sutherland:

So you were David's father,
And he was your only son. . .

Oh, the letters that he wrote you,
And I can see them still,
Not a word of the fighting
But just the sheep on the hill. . .

You were only David's father,
But I had fifty sons
When we went up in the evening
Under the arch of the guns,
And we came back at twilight –
Oh God! I heard them call

---

(52) *The London Gazette*, 24th June 1916

To me for help and pity
That could not help at all.[53]

A thread of youthful paternalism runs through this poem, but it is, nevertheless, a striking testament of Mackintosh's empathy for his Highland comrades, and for the responsibility he felt on leading them. He had obviously gained an insight into Sutherland's background when censoring his letters home, which was one of his duties as an officer.

The poem is written like a Gaelic lament, or *coronach*: this is not accidental, as he refers to the '*coronach* for Christ' in Act II of 'The Remembered Gods', and knew its style. David was not an only son, a brother James served in the Machine Gun Corps. Perhaps Mackintosh did not know about him, or was exercising poetic licence, to contrast with his fifty sons.

The *John O' Groat Journal* of 26th May 1916[54] carried a full casualty list for the raid together with a report on it sent by Captain Sutherland, who wrote for the newspaper as 'Northern Eye-Witness'. His account later formed the basis of the relevant section in his book *The War Diary of the 5th Seaforth Highlanders*. The list was as follows (some names were wrongly spelled):

> Killed.
> Killed – Pte. D. Sutherland (Reay), C Coy.
> Killed in our own trenches after returning, by the bursting of a bomb in his haversack – Pte. MacDowell, C. Coy. (Belfast).
> Died of wounds in hospital – Pts. A. Macdonald, D. Coy. (Skye) and Pte. A. Thompson, C. Coy. (Belfast).
> Wounded.
> 2nd Lieutenant. C.E. Mackay – right arm, not serious.
> Pte. O. Burns, C. Coy (Belfast) gunshot wounds on head and body, serious.
> Pte. K. Macleod, A. Coy (Lochinver) – back and abdomen wounds, serious.
> Pte. J. Hastings, C. Coy – wounds on leg and back, serious.

---

(53) *A Highland Regiment*, ibid, page 40

(54) *John O' Groat Journal* per Ally Budge

Pte. R. F. Harper, C. Coy. (Breadalbane Terrace, Wick) – face
    wounds, not serious.
Pte. J. Mackintosh, A. Coy. (Melvich) – thigh and fingers,
    not serious.
Sergt. J. Sinclair, B. Coy. (Brora) – head and right hand,
    not serious.
Pte. J. Corbett, B. Coy. (Kinlochbervie) – legs and arms,
    not serious.
Sergt. R.N. Morrison, A. Coy. (Kinlochbervie) – left temple,
    not serious.
Pte. A. C. Macdonald, A. Coy. (Essex) – face – not serious.
Pte. R. F. Johnstone, B. Coy. (Thurso) – hip and arm,
    not serious.
Pte. D. Sutherland, A. Coy. (Backies, Golspie) – right arm,
    slight.

On 2nd June the *John O' Groat Journal* contained the following
item about Private Sutherland, which mentions his background and
his youth – since he joined up near the beginning of the war and was
nineteen[55] when he died, he must have been under age on enlistment:

> Last week the casualty list in connection with the
> brilliant raid by the Caithness and Sutherland
> Territorials included the loss of Pte. D. Sutherland,
> Dounreay, whose loss is both keenly felt and deeply
> regretted by the community. Pte. Sutherland, who was
> the son of Sinclair Sutherland, landholder Dounreay
> enlisted at the beginning of the war despite his youth. In
> November last year he was drafted abroad and after
> serving his country in a manner which should mingle
> pride with the grief of his relatives, he has nobly fallen
> on the field of battle. His parents have received a letter
> of condolence from his officer and the chaplain, each of
> whom testifies to the esteem in which the deceased lad
> was held, amongst his comrades.'

Though David Sutherland has no know grave, he is commemorated on Bay 8 of the Arras and also in Reay where he is included

---

(55) Age given on family grave stone in Reay churchyard

on the village war memorial, on the Roll of Honour in the village hall, as well as on the family memorial stone in Reay churchyard which directs readers to the poem 'In Memoriam'.

Mackintosh's letter to the family of Pte. Andrew Thompson in Belfast was printed in the *Belfast Evening Telegraph* of 6th June, which also contained the announcement of his death: the previous day's edition had printed Pte. McDowell's. The quotation from Mackintosh's letter to Thomson's widow reads:

> Your husband was wounded by a mortar bomb whilst taking part in a raid on the German trenches. Both his legs were badly injured, and he was otherwise badly battered. He behaved with great gallantry, and I never wish to see a more heroic soldier.

His letter counters the assumption that officers' letters to relatives were all tactfully phrased to avoid further pain to the reader: 'badly battered' is blunt, without being over descriptive and reflects an unwillingness on Mackintosh's behalf to conceal the harsh realities of war. The 5th Seaforths had had a recruiting office in Belfast, near the docks, which is why Belfast men came to be members of a Highland Regiment.

Pte. Thompson was buried in Aubigny Communal Cemetery Extension (Plot1, Row B, Grave 59), and Pte. McDowell was buried at Maroeuil, in the British Cemetery (Plot 1, Row E, Grave 13), which is in the adjacent row to the grave of Lance Corporal Macdonald (Row D, Grave 12).[56] Mackintosh could even have been present when the latter two comrades were laid to rest. There is no doubt, in any case, that he never forgot them, and felt a continuing obligation to their memory. Many years afterwards, when families were given the opportunity to have an inscription chosen by them carved on the headstones which eventually replaced the wooden crosses on soldiers' graves, the family of Lance Corporal Macdonald, who came from Stenschall, near Staffin, on the Isle of Skye, chose the following excerpt from Paraphrase 53 in the old Gaelic Psalter and Hymnary:[57]

---

(56) C.W.G.C. Soldiers Died in the Great War, ibid

(57) Translation by Margaret MacQuarrie, Plockton

FOS TAMULL BEAG IS RUIGIDH SINN AN CALADH
AIT FADEOIDH
(YET A LITTLE WHILE AND WE SHALL REACH
THE JOYOUS HARBOUR AT LAST)

They were confident of being reunited after death. By contrast, in the poem 'Ship of the Soul' written in 1917, Mackintosh saw no satisfactory end to his wanderings, even after death.

The raid was the most severe personal and military challenge so far faced by Mackintosh; he survived, but dealing with the consequent combination of grief and renown must have been very difficult.

David Sutherland, subject of
'In Memoriam'

Sergeant Goddard

WHERE THE TRENCHES RUN DOWN FROM THE SOMME TO THE SEA
Tune – 'The Mountains of Mourne'

Oh, Mary the front is a wonderful place,
Where a person can't fight without shaving his face;
We're not frightened of shells, so I've found,
But when generals come near we all get to ground.
I met one in a trench, and some tea-leaves were there,
And we got such a strafing it whitened our hair,
So it seems we must swallow the leaves in our tea,
Where the trenches run down from the Somme to the sea.

At night-time I can't sleep a full minute's space,
For the rats playing games on the top of my face,
And other small creatures I'd rather not name,
But they live in the folds of my kilt just the same.
Tell wee Jimmy, if only our dug-out he knew,
He'd never be asking to go to the Zoo.
For every dug-out is a menagerie,
Where the trenches stretch down from the Somme to the sea.

The sap that I stand in, it nightly is made
Into hell by a thing they call Rifle Grenade,
And when heavy mortars are bursting close by
It is not light of battle that gleams in my eye.
Don't think me a coward though, Mary, my dear,
For along the whole front it's the same thing I fear,
And every young hero is funking like me,
Where the trenches run down from the Somme to the sea.

At Albert they've lately begun an advance
Which is going to shove all the Bosches out of France,
And we are all waiting and hoping some day
To meet with the gentleman over the way.
And oh, what a state of delight we'll be in
When we're bombing our way up the streets of Berlin,
So I hope in a few months I surely shall be
In a train running down from Berlin to the sea.

War, The Liberator

PEACE UPON EARTH

Under the sky of battle, under the arch of the guns,
Where in the mad red torrent the river of fighting runs,
Where the shout of a strong man sounds no more than
                    a broken groan,
And the heart of man rejoicing stands up in its strength alone,
There is the hour of trial; and when the battle is spent,
And we sit drinking together, laughing and well content,
Deep in my heart I am hearing a little still voice that sings,
'Well, but what will you do when there comes
                    an end of these things?'

Laughter, hard drinking and fighting, quarrels of friend and friend,
The eyes of the men that trust us, of all these there is end.
No more in the raving barrage in one swift clamorous breath
We shall jest and curse together on the razor-edge of death.
Old ways, old ways, old comrades, for ever and ever good-bye!
We shall walk no more in the twisted ways of the trenches, you and I,
For nations have heard the tidings, they have sworn that
                    wars shall cease,
And it's all one damned long Sunday walk down the straight, flat
                    road of peace.

Yes, we shall be raptured again by the frock-coat's singular charm,
That goes so well with children and a loving wife on your arm,
Treading a road that is paved with family dinner and teas,
A sensible dull suburban road planted with decorous trees,
Till we come at last to the heaven our peaceable saints have trod,
Like the sort of church that our fathers built and called it
                    the house of God,
And a God like a super-bishop in an apron and nice top-hat –
O, God, you are God of battles. Forbid that we come to that!

God, you are God of soldiers, merry and rough and kind,
Give to your sons an earth and a heaven more to our mind,
Meat and drink for the body, laughter and song for the soul,
And fighting and quick clean death to end and complete the whole.
Never a hope of heaven, never a fear of hell,
Only the knowledge that you are a soldier, and all is well,
And whether the end be death or a merrier life be given,
We shall have died in the pride of our youth –
                              and that will be heaven.

On the road to Fricourt, 1916
A Highland Regiment

HIGH WOOD TO WATERLOT FARM
Tune – 'Chalk Farm to Camberwell Green'

There is a wood at the top of a hill,
If it's not shifted it's standing there still;
There is a farm a short distance away,
But I'd not advise you to go there by day,
For the snipers abound, and the shells are not rare,
And a man's only chance is to run like a hare,
So take my advice if you're chancing your arm
From High Wood to Waterlot Farm.

Chorus –
High Wood to Waterlot Farm,
All on a summer's day,
Up you get to the top of the trench
Though you're sniped at all the way,
If you've got a smoke helmet there
You'd best put it on if you could
For the wood down by Waterlot Farm
Is a bloody high wood.

War, The Liberator

RECRUITING

'Lads, you're wanted, go and help,'
On the railway carriage wall
Stuck the poster, and I thought
Of the hands that penned the call.

Fat civilians wishing they
'Could go out and fight the Hun.'
Can't you see them thanking God
That they're over forty-one?

Girls with feathers, vulgar songs –
Washy verse on England's need –
God – and don't we damned well know
How the message ought to read.

'Lads, you're wanted! over there,'
Shiver in the morning dew,
More poor devils like yourselves
Waiting to be killed by you.

Go and help to swell the names
In the casualty lists.
Help to make a column's stuff
For the blasted journalists.

Help to keep them nice and safe
From the wicked German foe,
Don't let him come over here!
'Lads, you're wanted-out you go.'

There's a better word than that,
Lads, and can't you hear it come,
From a million men that call
You to share their martyrdom.

Leave the harlots still to sing
Comic songs about the Hun,
Leave the fat old men to say
Now *we've* got them on the run.

Better twenty honest years
Than their dull three score and ten.
Lads, you're wanted. Come and learn
To live and die with honest men.

You shall learn what men can do
If you will but pay the price,
Learn the gaiety and strength
In the gallant sacrifice.

Take your risk of life and death
Underneath the open sky.
Live clean or go out quick –
Lads, you're wanted. Come and die.

War, The Liberator

CHAPTER 5

HIGH WOOD July 1916

The wild war pipes were calling,
Our hearts were blithe and free
When we went up the valley
To the death we could not see.

'To the Highland Division', High Wood
A Highland Regiment

I n early July 1916 Mackintosh wrote 'Where the trenches run down from the Somme to the Sea', to the tune of 'The Mountains of Mourne'. Its last verse begins:[1]

At Albert they've lately begun an advance
Which is going to shove all the Bosches out of France,
And oh, what a state of delight we'll be in
When we're bombing our way up the streets of Berlin.

The song has all the innocent optimism of uninformed early July 1916. After two years of vain assaults the British thought that they had the recipe for success: guns and shells were available on a limitless scale, and the preliminary bombardment pounded the Germans for seven days. There was ample fresh manpower, and every man was a volunteer and highly motivated and optimistic. The nation was impatient for success, and the 'Big Push' had been eagerly anticipated in the press, pubs, billets and headquarters. The illusion that open warfare could be resumed persisted, and the Somme offensive was expected to achieve this. Mackintosh's expectation that Berlin was a possibility in 1916 was widely shared.

---

(1) Page 96, *War, The Liberator*, E.A.Mackintosh. John Lane, The Bodley Head, 1918

Cavalry were in the rear to exploit the planned infantry break-through.

The 5th Seaforths had not taken part in any major offensive in the previous twelve months: they had sustained the discomfort, boredom, fear and casualties of normal trench warfare, enlivened by raids and mining by either side. Casualties in four months in the Labyrinth had not been severe:

> we have kept 'the luck of the Fifth' for our total
> casualties have been: 2 officers wounded, 16 men killed
> and 83 wounded, a much smaller list than the other
> battalions in the brigade.[2]

When the parody was written the battalion was not expecting to be sent to the Somme. Its front line had been stretched on 31st May to allow other divisions to move to the Somme:

> To prevent the Boche finding out that our brigade had
> extended its front, the units of the 152nd Brigade had
> their kilts and Balmoral bonnets taken from them and
> had been fitted out with khaki trousers and field service
> caps, much to the disgust of the men, who, suspicious of
> some Sassenach plot to strip them for ever of the kilt,
> grumbled very much and protested to their officers.[3]

On 14th July the Division was relieved. The Labyrinth had been unpleasant in the extreme, and the feelings of the 51st Highland Division as it withdrew from it are summed up by Captain R.B. Ross, of the 7th Gordons:[4]

> . . . our eyes, which for many months had never gazed
> upon an intact roof, or a field that was not cursed with
> shells or sanctified with crosses, or a tree that was not
> blasted or decaying, now witnessed villages unsullied by

---

(2) Page 71, *War Diary of the 5th Seaforth Highlanders*, Capt. D.Sutherland. John Lane, 1920

(3) Sutherland, ibid, page 69

(4) Page 212, *The Fifty-First in France* Capt. R.B.Ross. Hodder and Stoughton, 1918

war, rich pasture, and abundant crops, and the broad
leafy avenues of Capelle, Aubigny and Savy.

On July 14th the 5th Seaforths travelled by lorry from billets in
Acq to Beaudricourt, then route marched to Autheux from where
they took a train to the railhead at Méricourt-Ribemont, a short
march from billets at Buire, in the rear of the battle: they arrived
there on 21st July. On the 22nd they bivouaced in open ground
near Fricourt as part of the divisional reserve: they would not be
committed to the initial assault carried out that day by the 154th
Brigade: they were to reinforce or exploit any advance.

Prior to this Mackintosh had been corresponding with A.E.J.
Rawlinson (Jack) and his mother, commiserating with them because
Jack's brother Godfrey ('Gogs'), a 21 year old Second Lieutenant
in the 1/4th Oxford and Buckinghamshire Light Infantry had died
from stomach wounds on July 16th. In a letter to Mackintosh on
31st July Rawlinson wrote:

> My Dear Alan,
> You had replied to my mother, and I owed you a line, but
> had been too pressed to write. . . Yes, I think Mother is
> bearing up very bravely. I am very glad to know of what she
> writes to you. I suppose as a regiment you chafe at not being
> in action: but I too am thankful that you are not.[5]

Rawlinson was not to know as he wrote that the 5th Seaforths
were already in the line.

To the poem 'Peace Upon Earth' was added the note 'On the
road to Fricourt': it must have been written in the days before the
battalion arrived at Fricourt, in billets, or on the train, and in
whatever mix of moods invades the mind of a man faced with
imminent battle.

Mackintosh contemplated the peace which would follow the war:[6]

---

(5) Letter from Jack Rawlinson to Mackintosh, 31/7/1916.
(Rosemary Beazley)

(6) Page 44, *A Highland Regiment*, E.A.Mackintosh. John Lane,
The Bodley Head, 1918

No more in the raving barrage in one swift clamorous breath
We shall jest and curse together on the razor edge of death. . .

We shall walk no more in the twisted ways of the trenches,
                                        you and I,
For the nations have heard the tidings, they have sworn
                                that war will cease,
And it's all one damned long Sunday walk down
                        the straight flat road of peace. . .

And whether the end be death or a merrier life be given,
We shall have died in the pride of our youth –
                                and that will be heaven.

There are no illusions about the awfulness of what has been,
and what lay ahead.

The apparent death wish implicit in 'To My Sister'[7] reappears.
Had he reached the stage where he thought that death was inevitable
to anyone at the Front, or was he simply coming to terms with the
likelihood of death, and trying to make the best of it? This might
be the case, were it not for his negative perception of post-war life
as 'one damned long Sunday walk down the straight, flat road of
peace.' Here he is reflecting the commonly held belief that the war
he was fighting was the war to end wars, and that endless peace
would follow it.

His ability to exercise the future's hindsight first showed in 'Old
Age',[8] in 1914, when he anticipated himself and his love, in old
age, looking back at the ineptness of their youthful relationship.
The same imaginative avenues are being explored on his way to
the Somme. Is there a wistful longing for the order of family life
and 'the Sunday walk'? He cannot indulge in this as he has learned
to live a day at a time, and fantasising about post-war life may divert
him from the business of war, and his personal survival. Does he
rail against quiet family life to enable himself to withstand the horror
of the approaching battle? Or is he simply recognising, as any
sensitive man would, that walking 'the razor's edge of death' will

(7) *A Highland Regiment*, ibid, page 38

(8) *A Highland Regiment*, ibid, page 88. See OXFORD poems

put a perspective on ordinary life which will make it seem dull by comparison?

The last line: 'we shall have died in the pride of our youth – and that will be heaven' may hold a key, that he did not want to be old: he disparages old civilians in 'Recruiting',[9] and with his bad eyesight, which might even then have been worsening, he may not have anticipated old age with any degree of optimism.

It is tempting to suggest that he had a death wish. Yet in 'In the Wood',[10] he records of himself: 'He was very afraid and most unwilling to die' yet his apparent courting of death, or accepting its near inevitability, emerges in many of his poems, and becomes more apparent in late 1916 and early 1917. The first sign of this apparent death wish had appeared in 'Before the Summer', (poems Chapter 3) at Corbie. If there had been a girl at home, it is less likely that he would have felt like this.

Having come to the Army as a lonely and disappointed man he had found humour, comradeship, mutual loyalty and trust in the battalion, and liked it. Because he had a sense of immortality it bound him to his colleagues, of all ranks, living or dead. He had not developed clinical detachment, which might have made the losses seem less personal. This inability, coupled with his sense of loyalty, at the expense of his will to live, may ultimately have killed him. The poem is a confusion of moods, lurching between a dream of peace, and a glorification of battle, the same kind of glorification that was found in 'To My Sister' when he steeled himself for the raid in the Labyrinth.

For a battalion expecting to take part in an offensive, it was to be a frustrating and punishing two weeks. On the 22nd they were in reserve in open ground near Fricourt: Captain Ross of the 7th Gordons mistakenly said that 'the brigade in reserve was in comfortable bivouac near Fricourt and Bécordel.'[11] But the 5th Seaforths had sustained seven wounded by shell fire, and shifted back for a day, before moving on the 24th to the west of Bécordel.

They were close to Bécordel Château, where they had been in 1915, and two of the battalion officers explored dug-outs which they had occupied the previous year. One recovered a bottle of

(9) *War, The Liberator*, ibid, page 15

(10) *War, The Liberator*, ibid, page 143

(11) Ross, ibid, page 221

whisky which he had hidden away eleven months before, and it was consumed in 'Faither's' dug-out: as 'Faither' was still Mackintosh's company commander it is reasonable to expect that he had his share!

'On the night of the 26th a move was made to Mametz Wood, a reserve position, but one more hated than the front line in High Wood.'[12] The 5th Seaforths were in support, with the rest of the 152nd Brigade, with the 153rd in the front line, having relieved the 154th Brigade, which had failed to take High Wood.

Mametz Wood was to the north west of Fricourt Wood. Between them lay the misnamed Happy Valley, which was the only route to the battle that was taking place for High Wood, the highest point on the battlefield. The Highland Division had been flung into the battle to take High Wood, with the 5th Division on its right and the 19th Division on its left. It was an unpleasant place to be. Captain Ross recorded:

> A giant of steel seemed to have ridden over the proud German defences. Villages were wiped completely out of existence; woods were laid waste. Saddest sight of all, there was not a blade of grass visible. A tumbled heap of rubble marked the spot where the church of Fricourt once stood. Its very gables were powdered to dust. A few gable ends still stood in Mametz. These were gradually being demolished by enemy fire. Trenches were everywhere blown out of recognition. Disrupted sand bags littered the broken earth. In every direction disused gunpits with piles of empty shell-cases showed how the artillery had advanced. A poignant reminder that victory is not purchased without cost lay in the mounds of newly delved earth where blue flags were fluttering over the dead.[13]

Bewsher states:

> For the most part the only protection the residents of the valley had against shell fire were slits cut in the ground covered with waterproof sheets or corrugated iron. Happy

(12) Sutherland, ibid, page 77

(13) Ross, ibid, page 221

146

Valley, with its dust and flies and its stench of half buried animals and men, will remain to all who knew it an ineffaceable memory.[14]

The war diary of the 5th Seaforths records:[15]

27.7 Mametz Wood. Battalion experienced hostile gas shelling during the early morning. Lt. Garry suffered from gas poisoning. 6 men killed, 31 O.R.s wounded and gassed. 3 missing (possibly wounded and in hospital).

28.7 Comparatively quiet day. Heavy shelling during the darkness.

29.7 Lt. Col. A. A. Spooner D.S.O. to 183 Brigade (promoted). 1 killed in action. 2nd Lt. MacKay J. shell shocked. 16 O.R.s wounded and shock.

30.7. Major Berry H.L.I. took over. Very heavy shelling during the afternoon. 6 men killed. Lt. Reader mortally wounded. Captain W.S.S.Harper and 2nd Lt. Kestin to hospital shell shock. 43 O.R.s wounded or shell shock.

31.7. Fatigue and working parties. Quieter than previous day.

1.8. Battalion in front line near High Wood on the left and stretching to the right. Enemy had the range of our trenches and intermittently bombarded our lines with shell fire effecting much damage on the right portion. During the night the enemy bombarded our lines almost continuously. Captain Dunn invalided to England.

2.8. Same as for 1.8., 3 men killed, 8 wounded. Into support at Bazentin le Grand.

Although the other two brigades of the Highland Division launched unsuccessful assaults on High Wood, the 152nd Brigade, containing the 5th Seaforths, did not go over the top. By the time

---

(14) Page 76, *The History of the 51st (Highland) Division*, F.W.Bewsher. Blackwood, 1921

(15) 5th Seaforths' battalion war diary. Q.O.H museum, Fort George, Inverness

the battalion moved into the line on 1st August, Mackintosh had probably been evacuated.

The war diary does not name Mackintosh as a casualty, although the 'Memoir' to him in *War, The Liberator* records that he was wounded and gassed at High Wood. The accuracy of the war diary depended on the writer having a few moments of peace and quiet to compile it, and having all the appropriate information available.

The wounding or death of six officers is shown in the war diary, yet ten officers are recorded as wounded or dead in Captain Sutherland's book.[16] The fates of four officers, including Mackintosh, are not entered. Evidence of the difficulty of keeping accurate records exists in the 27.7 entry '3 missing (possibly in hospital)': another possibility is that they had been obliterated by a direct hit. The 1st August entry states that the 5th Seaforths' position in Mametz Wood was severely bombarded, but no casualties are noted. The 2nd August entry records the same shelling and notes casualties. It is unlikely that there were none on 1st August. July 31st was a quiet day, one which should have allowed accurate recording of officer casualties, yet Mackintosh was not noted. July 30th was a bad day, and this is the one on which Mackintosh was wounded.

Mackintosh wrote a prose account of this event, 'In The Wood'. As in 'The Raid', he changed the names: he features as the Subaltern and 'MacTaggart':[17]

> The tall trees stood up parched and blasted by the hot
> breath of the explosions or lay where the explosions had
> struck them down; the fallen leaves were littered in the
> hollows, whence rose, if you disturbed them, an acrid
> smell of gas launched over the woods four days before
> and everywhere among the undergrowth and the fallen
> trees ran a network of narrow trenches and shallow
> burrows from which rose the sound of talk and the smell
> of cooking, the resting place of the supports who were to
> be ready that night to move up through the valley and
> sweep past the victorious front-line brigade into an
> enemy village two miles away.

(16) Sutherland, ibid, page 79

(17) *War, The Liberator*, ibid, page 143ff

An enemy plane flew over, then shelling began:

. . . The Subaltern saw the mess dixie hurled into a
bush, and the terrified man beside him darted his head
into a little hole at the side of the trench. Over the
Subaltern came the bombardment feeling; a sensation
which mingles a curious numbness of all ordinary
emotions with an abounding pride and a complete
contempt for anyone more frightened than oneself; he
turned slowly to the man and told him to take his head
out of the hole. . .
I don't know if I have given you the impression that the
subaltern was a fearless young gentlemen; but, if so, it
was not my intention. He was very afraid and most
unwilling to die, and he showed it, if the men had only
noticed, by his nervous movement of relief after each
close burst. A somewhat vigorous self control, combined
with a very real pleasure at being so close to death and
alive, enabled him to delude the privates; but inside he
was quaking . . .

The barrage moved on:

The Subaltern felt that he ought to get out, but somehow
he couldn't. What if the barrage started again and caught
him in the open? He climbed out and stood ready to jump
down if another shell came. From the next trench stretcher
bearers moved towards him looking for wounded. Almost
beside him a man lay in a dabble of blood; you would have
thought him asleep until you saw half his head lying beside
him cut neatly off by a big piece of shell. Farther over they
had dug out the buried men, but only one was alive. The
Corporal, who had worked so gallantly in the bombardment, collapsed suddenly with twitching hands and staring,
frightened eyes, proclaiming the shell shock he had held
off while the work had to be done. Stretcher bearers came,
carrying broken moaning wounded. The Subaltern,
ashamed by their calm, braced himself and stepped into
the open.

There he met another Sub. helping along a Captain, an old friend of his. MacTaggart greeted him cheerily, and was answered by a hopeless stare and a writhing mouth trying in vain to form words. The captain was dumb.[18] 'That last 8 inch burst almost on him,' the other Subaltern explained. 'All the men with him were killed, and he's got it badly. Come on, Willie, it's all right now.'

The dumb man mumbled piteously and cringed to the ground as a shell whined over. The two started to take him along to the Aid Post but every movement was difficult to his uncontrolled limbs, and every sound a torture to the bewildered brain. It was a long time before they got there, and when they did, the Aid Post was like a shambles with blood and wounded men. The two slung their friend down to the doctor, and went to report him a casualty at Headquarters next door. There the C.O. met them with operation orders for the attack that night, and a request that MacTaggart would take certain messages to other companies. . .

As MacTaggart crossed the open ground he was gripped with a sudden fear. The whining and crash of shells was coming nearer again, and he had two companies to see before he could get back to his own burrow. He ran hastily to the first Coy. H.Q., then paused there, bracing himself for his next rush, for the barrage was on their lines again, although not so heavily. Out he ran and along to the next H.Q., fixing his mind on the job, and not allowing himself to think of shells, when a low shrapnel, beautifully timed, burst close beside him, knocking him over; picking himself up he staggered to the trench and handed over the message, only conscious of a sudden quiet, for that shrapnel had been the last of the barrage. Then he found his mouth full of blood, and his limbs weak and tottering. He was not wounded, he knew; but supposed it must be shell shock.

At Headquarters he reported the messages delivered, and got some opium from the doctor; in a dream he got some rum,

---

(18) 5th Seaforths' battalion war diary, ibid. Note: this was possibly Captain W.S.S.Harper

then his own men, and found new vigour in his limbs and ferocity in his mind. 'Go down? I'm damned if I will,' he muttered, and walked along the trench. The British barrage was on now, and the troops were all ready to move up.

Mackintosh was afraid that the replacements would not do well in the forthcoming battle. Their reaction reflects the enormous cultural and changes that have taken place in society since 1916.

In the trench he found the other officers and knew that they were thinking the same. 'The old hands ought to help them on,' said his Captain doubtfully. 'But I wish we hadn't lost so many today. It'll shake them up a bit.'
'What is today?' asked MacTaggart inconsequently, 'Sunday, isn't it?' A voice from a private echoed his question a little way along. There was a buzz of conversation then suddenly a hush. The strong voice of a sergeant was lifted up in the shaking lilt of an old Psalm tune.
'My God,' breathed the Subaltern, as the other voices joined in. 'They're the old gang yet.'

He took me from the fearful pit
And from the miry clay,
And on the rock he set my feet,
Establishing my way.

The Psalm ended; another voice said, 'I'll give you a grand one for this day, boys,' and once again the strong rough voices rang out through the woods, grim earnestness in every tone:

Now Israel may say, and that truly
If that the Lord had not been on our side,
If that the Lord had not our cause maintained
When cruel men against us furiously
Rose up in wrath to make of us their prey.

A runner came up to them with a message. The captain read it, and stood up, shaking his equipment on to his

shoulders. From the valley below came the roar of the
German barrage, but over it rose the psalm:

Therefore our trust is in the Lord his name
Who heaven and earth by his own power did frame.

There was a sudden silence and a shout from the Captain.
'Get on you equipment, men. We're to move up now,' and
the officers strolled to their platoons with light hearts.
Whatever happened they knew the men would follow them.
The spirit of the regiment was still the same.

As there is no note of Mackintosh being wounded or shell-
shocked in the war diary, it is reasonable to suppose that he collapsed
at the end of the events featured in 'In The Wood'. He had been
blown over by blast, emerged from it tottering and weak-limbed,
and bleeding from the mouth, and relates that he was not wounded,
and thought that it might be shell shock. He undoubtedly suffered
from the blast of the explosion, and he may have sustained shrapnel
injuries of which he was unaware, due to shock. Or his leg may
have been badly twisted when he was blown off his feet. His letters
to his publisher later in the year indicate a leg and eye injury.

I'm still here with my leg pretty bad and one of my eyes
almost blind. 2.11.16.
My eyes are possibly going blind. 7.11.16
My leg's giving me the jumps these days.' 11.1.17
I'm a cripple again – 11.2.17[19]

His acceptance of opium at the Aid Post suggests that he was
hurt by the blast, as it was then prescribed as a pain killer, and his
consumption of rum would meet the need to revive his spirits: he
was 'in a dream' and his muttered refusals to 'go down' would have
been a reaction to advice from the medical officer or his fellow
officers to go back. The adrenalin rush which kept him on his feet
may simply have drained away after a time.

A less dramatic possibility is that he might simply have tripped

---

(19) The Bodley Head Collection, Harry Ransom Humanities
Research Center, University of Texas at Austin

into a trench or shell hole and been knocked unconscious and found later by stretcher bearers.

Apart from 'In The Wood', which refers to his injuries, the only other evidence is in the 'Memoir'. Mackintosh must have told John Murray himself that he had been gassed and wounded, for the information in the 'Memoir' in *War, The Liberator* could only have come from Mackintosh, or from people very close to him. The unit had been subjected to gas shells on 27th July, but only Lt. Garry is listed as having suffered gas poisoning.[20]

Although the war diary does not record gas shelling again the 'enemy shelled Happy Valley mercilessly day and night, an intense barrage of high explosive, air bursts and gas shells being placed completely across it at irregular intervals, and moving backwards and forwards, up and down it.'[21] Gas shells were frequent enough to irritate and be unremarked upon unless they were concentrated, as they were on July 27th. There was certainly gas in the small hours of 31st July, when the 5th Seaforths were still in Mametz Wood.[22]

A further possibility is that Mackintosh was simply shell-shocked, as he himself recognised. Whilst he and his brother officers recognised the condition and did not condemn it, the General Staff and the civilian population was not so understanding. Given his self-image in his poems and prose pieces as a man elated by conquering his fear, and already possessing an M.C., it would not be easy for him to admit publicly to shell shock. However, his letters to his publisher mention specific physical defects, so, although he may have suffered shock as an immediate result of the incident, it is unlikely that he suffered from prolonged shock.

Collapse as a delayed result of the shrapnel burst, either from shock, or through exhaustion or an accident, appears to be the most likely outcome of the day, maybe just after the events in 'In The Wood'. He may have collapsed into a pocket of low lying gas, and lain there for a time before being discovered. Given the lack of written evidence, all is speculation.

He makes no reference at all to the death of his friend Lt. Reader,

---

(20) 5th Seaforths' battalion war diary. Q.O.H. museum, Fort George, Inverness

(21) Bewsher, ibid, page 74

(22) Page 91, *A Medico's Luck in the Great War*, David Rorie. Milne and Hutchison, Aberdeen, 1929

whom he mourns in 'On Vimy Ridge', written in the autumn of 1916. Reader's mortal wound must have occurred when Mackintosh was no longer in a position to be aware of it, or he may not have missed him in the confusion caused by the bombardments.

The impression at the conclusion of 'In The Wood' is that the battalion was moving into action in support of that day's attack on High Wood. This was the intention, but the reality is that the 5thSeaforths stayed where they were, because the attack failed, and that another twenty-four hours elapsed before they moved forward to relieve the depleted units in the front line.

Either Mackintosh knew that the battalion stayed where it was and decided to conclude the story in an heroic vein to give it dramatic effect, or his knowledge of the circumstances ended with collapse immediately after the order to move was given – then countermanded.

There was a well-established casualty evacuation system. The Regimental Aid Posts, where First Aid was administered, were serviced by the battalion medical officer and stretcher bearers. The stretcher bearers from the Royal Army Medical Corps Field Ambulance then carried the wounded back, or pushed them on wheeled stretchers, to the Collecting Post.

Horse-drawn wagons or motor ambulances moved them to the Advanced Dressing Station, then they went by motor ambulance to the Main Dressing Station. All medical care to this point was provided by the Highland Division's R.A.M.C. Thereafter the wounded went to the Casualty Clearing Station and Base Hospital, before being sent home, or returned to the front.

There was a Collecting Post in a quarry at the High Wood end of Happy Valley, through which Mackintosh might have been evacuated:[23]

> . . . on the evening of the 30th, the corner – 'Death Corner' – on the Mametz side of the quarry became impossible for cars (motor ambulances), owing to the shell holes; so horse ambulance wagons worked past it by the field track, and for three days and nights took the stretcher cases from the quarry all the way to the top of the hill at Mametz, where they were reloaded in the

(23) Rorie, ibid, page 89

motor ambulances to go back to the A.D.S. at the file
factory, Bécordel.

One of these trips is described by a horse transport driver:[24]

> If I remember aright the 153rd Brigade went over the
> top that night, so we had our work cut out to keep the
> Quarry Post clear . . . we jogged along not too badly
> until about 2 a.m. (31.7.16) . . . we got to the quarry all
> right, loaded up and started on our return journey.
> About a hundred yards from Death Corner a Gordon
> picket stopped us and told us that we should not go any
> further as the road was being heavily shelled. As,
> however, we had a serious case on board and the
> patients were 'windy', we decided to push on. At the
> corner we could not see a yard in front of us for gas and
> mist, and it was no easy job guiding the wagon through
> a maze of shell holes.
> Suddenly a great shell burst twenty yards from us, and
> my leader, thinking it was to the left, swerved to the
> right to avoid the hole. As it happened the swerve took
> us right into it and the wagon turned over on its side. . .
> Stuck in a shell hole, the enemy shelling and the valley
> full of gas: no wagon orderly and several badly wounded
> men inside whom we were unable to help – what were we
> to do? The leader unhitched a horse and rode off to
> Mametz for help while I stuck to the wagon. . .
> Back came the leader no better than when he had left:
> not a soul at Mametz could help us. I then went off for a
> try, and came back with no better luck. When we had
> about given up hope, one of our own ambulance wagons
> arrived on the scene from the Quarry. They pluckily
> drew up alongside and we got our cases out of the
> capsized wagon through the canvas sides and laid them
> on the ground, while their wagon went off at the gallop
> for Mametz and came back again for them, loaded up
> and set off again up the valley. . .
> I must say it was a trying experience.

---

(24) Rorie, ibid, pages 90ff

The brief war diary entries do not capture the flavour of the day in the same way as 'In The Wood' or the R.A.M.C drivers' account: the diary's terseness indicates that survival was the order of the day, and form filling would be accorded low priority. The confusion of battle, and the fog of war, makes the precise identification of Mackintosh's wounding and evacuation an impossibility.[25]

Apart from 'In The Wood' there are only two other references to High Wood in Mackintosh's poetry. Parodying 'Chalk Farm to Camberwell Green' he wrote 'High Wood to Waterlot Farm.' It adopts the same approach to the hazards of daily trench life as is found in 'Where the trenches run down from the Somme to the sea', trying to make fun of being a target for a sniper or of being gassed:[26]

Up you get to the top of the trench
Though you're sniped at all the way.
If you've got a smoke helmet there
You'd best put it on if you could,
For the wood down by Waterlot Farm
Is a bloody high wood.

Later in the year, in November, celebrating the capture of Beaumont Hamel by the Highland Division, he recalled the misery and disappointment of the battle in 'High Wood, July – August 1916':[27]

Gay and gallant were we
On the day that we set forth,
But broken, broken, broken,
Is the valour of the North.

The thin lines stumbled forward
The dead and dying lay.
By the unseen death that caught us

---

(25) Correspondence with Rosemary Beazley

(26) *War, The Liberator*, ibid, page 101

(27) *War, The Liberator*, ibid, page 25

By the bullets' raging hail
Broken, broken, broken
Is the pride of the Gael.

The poem's significance is in the contrast between the optimism and the reality, but more so in Mackintosh's easy transfer of loyalty from his own battalion to the Highland Division. While Mackintosh's battalion was caught by the 'unseen death', the stumbling 'thin lines' belonged to other battalions of the division. This was a characteristic of the First World War, where the scale of operations almost reduced battalions to numerical and military insignificance, and made the divisions the key battlefield formations.

Being wounded in the battle for High Wood was the culmination of a year's service on the Western Front for Mackintosh. He had endured the monotony, squalor and danger of trench warfare, had reconnoitred and raided across No Man's Land, sustained bombardments, and seen his men and fellow officers die. He had been denied the chance of going over the top in a major offensive.

Whether he regretted this or not is not known. His evacuation from the battlefield in July 1916 gave him more than a year of life, which he might not have enjoyed had he remained with the battalion. It was a fruitful year, in which he published his first anthology, trained a cadet battalion in bombing, and met the woman he planned to marry.

ON VIMY RIDGE

On Vimy Ridge four months ago
We lived and fought my friends and I,
And watched the kindly dawn come slow,
Peace bringing from the eastern sky.
Now I sit in a quiet town
Remembering how I used to go
Among the dug-outs up and down,
On Vimy Ridge four months ago.

And often sitting here I've seen,
As then I saw them every night,
The friendly faces tired and keen
Across the flickering candle-light,
And heard their laughter gay and clear,
And watched the fires of courage glow,
Above the scattered ash of fear,
On Vimy Ridge four months ago.

Oh, friends of mine, where are you now?
Somewhere beneath the troubled sky,
With earth above the quiet brow,
Reader and Stalk for ever lie.
But dead or living out or here
I see the friends I used to know,
And hear the laughter gay and clear,
On Vimy Ridge four months ago.

A Highland Regiment

IN MEMORIAM
R.M.STALKER.MISSING, SEPTEMBER 1916

As I go down the highway,
  And through the village street
I hear the pipers playing
  And the tramp of marching feet.
The men I worked and fought with
  Swing by me four on four,
And at the end you follow
  Whom I shall see no more.

Oh, Stalk, where are you lying?
  Somewhere and far away,
Enemy hands have buried
  Your quiet contemptuous clay.
There was no greeting given,
  No tear of friend for friend,
From us when you flew over
  Exultant to the end.

I couldn't see the paper,
  I couldn't think that you
Would never walk the highway
  The way you used to do.
I turn at every footfall,
  Half-hoping, half-afraid
To see you coming, later
  Than usual for parade.

The old Lairg clique is broken,
  I drove there yesterday,
And the car was full of ghosts that sat
  Beside me all the way.

Ghosts of old songs and laughter,
   Ghosts of the jolly three,
That went the road together
   And go no more with me.

Oh, Stalk, but I am lonely,
   For all the days we knew,
And the bed on the floor at Lesdos
   We slept in, I and you.
The joyful nights in billets
   We laughed and drank and swore –
But the candle's burned out, Stalk,
   In the mess at Henancourt.

The candle's burned out now, old man,
   And the dawn's come grey and cold,
And I sit by the fire here
   Alone and sad and old.
Though all the rest come back again,
   You lie in a foreign land,
And the strongest link of all the chain
   Is broken in my hand.

A Highland Regiment

THE VOLUNTEER

I took my heart from the fire of love,
  Molten and warm not yet shaped clear,
And tempered it to steel of proof
  Upon the anvil block of fear.

With steady hammer-strokes I made
  A weapon ready for the fight,
And fashioned like a dagger-blade
  Narrow and pitiless and bright.

Cleanly and tearlessly it slew,
  But as the heavy days went on
The fire that once had warmed it grew
  Duller, and presently was gone.

Oh, innocence and lost desire,
  I strive to kindle it in vain,
Dead embers of a greying fire.
  I cannot melt my heart again.

A Highland Regiment

BEAUMONT-HAMEL
Captured, November 16th, 1916

1

Dead men at Beaumont
In the mud and rain,
You that were so warm once,
Flesh and blood and brain,
You've made an end of dying,
Hurts and cold and crying,
And all but quiet lying
Easeful after pain.

2

Dead men at Beaumont,
Do you dream at all
When the leaves of summer
Ripen to their fall?
Will you walk the heather,
Feel the Northern weather,
Wind and sun together,
Hear the grouse-cock call?

3

Maybe in the night-time
A shepherd boy will see,
Dead men, and ghastly,
Kilted to the knee,
Fresh from new blood-shedding,
With airy footsteps treading,
Hill and field and steading,
Where they used to be.

4

Nay, not so I see you
Dead friends of mine;
But like a dying pibroch
From the battle-line,
I hear your laughter ringing,
And the sweet songs you're singing,
And the keen words winging
Across the smoke and wine.

5

So we shall see you,
Be it peace or war,
Still in all adventures
You shall go before,
And our children dreaming,
Shall see you bayonets gleaming,
Scotland's warriors streaming
Forward evermore.

War, The Liberator

FROM HOME
TO THE MEN WHO FELL AT BEAUMONT-HAMEL
November 13th 1916

The pale sun woke in the eastern sky
And a veil of moist was drawn
Over the faces of death and fame
When you went up in the dawn.
With never a thought of death or fame,
Only the work to do,
When you went over the top, my friends,
And I not there with you.

The veil is rent with a rifle-flash
And shows me plain to see
Battle and bodies of men that lived
And fought along with me.
Oh God! It would not have been so hard
If I'd been in it too,
But you are lying stiff, my friends,
And I not there with you.

So here I sit in a pleasant room
By a comfortable fire,
With every thing that a man could want,
But not the heart's desire.
So I sit thinking and dreaming still,
A dream that won't come true,
Of you in the German trench, my friends,
And I not there with you.

War, The Liberator

TO BASIL, A BAVARIAN BOMBER
IN MEMORY OF THE BARRICADES IN THE LABYRINTH

In that remembered and unpleasant spot,
Where 'twas my task to haunt the barricade,
To hurl a bomb and give it to you hot
For every tiny sound you made.
Oh, Basil, when at first your bombs returned
Our martial spirits quickened and we burned
To land you one-the very batman yearned
For that decease of yours too long delayed.

And it was very galling, when we threw
Grenades that might have chilled the stoutest's blood,
Only to hear a plaintive call from you,
Informing us it was another dud.
And when the gent from Brigade was nigh,
Watching our Millses' fizzing through the sky,
To see you hit him neatly in the eye
With well-aimed lumps of harmless mud.

Often men have come to me and said that they
Had done you in at last and heard you yell,
But 'twas my sorrow on th'ensuing day
To hear again the voice I knew so well.
And when one night with dark and fell design
We carried out that raid upon your line,
It was with hopes, old enemy of mine,
That we should send you rapidly to hell.

But now that I am far from war's alarms
I like to muse upon the years to come
When we shall both have done with force and arms,
And Mills and Spaeter[1] will alike be dumb,
And those familiar accents I shall hear,
And we shall meet, oh peerless grenadier –
What shall it be, my Basil? Whisky? Beer?
Or punch concocted out of ration rum?

I think it shall be punch; I also think
That, as we ladle down the potent brew,
Myself and you, my Basil, ought to drink
Health to the barricades at which we threw
The bomb, a much less dangerous affair,
And I at last shall down you; for whate'er
Impotent things my poor old Millses were,
My punch is not a dud, I promise you.'

War, The Liberator

(1) Karl Spaeter, a prominent Bosche munitioneer

THREE BATTLES TO THE 51ST DIVISION

HIGH WOOD
July-August 1916

Oh gay were we in spirit
In the hours of the night
When we lay at rest at Albert
And waited for the fight;
Gay and gallant were we
On the day that we set forth,
But broken, broken, broken
Is the valour of the North.

The wild warpipes were calling,
Our hearts were blithe and free
When we went up the valley
To the death we could not see.
Clear lay the wood before us
In the clear summer weather,
But broken, broken, broken
Are the sons of the heather.

In the cold of the morning,
In the burning of the day,
The thin lines stumbled forward,
The dead and lying lay.
By the unseen death that caught us
By the bullets' raging hail
Broken, broken, broken
Is the pride of the Gael.

BEAUMONT-HAMEL
November 16th, 1916

But the North shall arise
Yet again in its strength;
Blood calling for blood
Shall be feasted at length.
For the dead men that lie
Underneath the hard skies,
For battle, for vengeance
The North shall arise.

In the cold of the morning
A grey mist was drawn
Over the waves
That went up in the dawn,
Went up like the waves
Of the wild Northern sea;
For the North has arisen,
The North has broke free.

Ghosts of the heroes
That died in the wood
Looked on the killing
And saw it was good.
Far over the hillsides
They saw in their dream
The kilted men charging,
The bayonets gleam.

By the cries that we heard,
By the things we had seen,
By the vengeance we took
In the bloody ravine,
By the men that we slew
In the mud and the rain,
The pride of the North
Has arisen again.

VICTORY AND FAILURE
ARRAS, April 9th
ROEUX, April 23rd, 1917

Not for the day of victory
I mourn I was not there,
The hard fierce rush of slaying men,
The hands up in the air,
But for the torn ranks struggling on
The old brave hopeless way,
The broken charge, the slow retreat,
And I so far away.

And listening to the tale of Roeux
I think I see again
The steady grim despairing ranks,
The courage and the pain,
The bodies of my friends that lie
Unburied in the dew –
Oh! friends of mine, and I not there
To die along with you.

War, The Liberator

FROM HOME
CAMBRIDGE

Here there is peace and easy living,
And a warm fire when the rain is driving,
There is no sound of strong men striving,
Here where the quiet waters flow,
But I am hearing the bullets ringing,
Hearing the great shells onward winging,
The dead men's voices are singing, singing,
   And I must rise and go.

Here there is ease and comfort for me,
A warm soft bed and a good roof o'er me
Here may be there is fame before me,
Honour and fame for all I know,
But I am seeing the thick rain falling,
Seeing the tired patrols out crawling,
The dead men's voices are calling, calling,
   And I must rise and go.

Back to the trench that I see so clearly,
Back to the fight I can see so nearly,
Back to the friends that I love so dearly,
The dead men lying amid the dew,
The droning sound of the great shells flying,
Filth and honour, and pain, and dying –
Dead friends of mine, oh, cease you crying,
   For I come back to you.

War, The Liberator

TO SYLVIA

Two months ago the skies were blue,
The fields were fresh and green,
And green the willow tree stood up,
With the lazy stream between.

Two months ago we sat and watched
The river drifting by –
And now – you're back at your work again
And here in a ditch I lie.

God knows – my dear – I did not want
To rise and leave you so,
But the dead men's hands were beckoning
And I knew that I must go.

The dead men's eyes were watching, lass,
Their lips were asking too,
We faced it out and paid the price –
Are we betrayed by you?

The days are long between, dear lass,
Before we meet again,
Long days of mud and work for me,
For you long care and pain.

But you'll forgive me yet, my dear,
Because of what you know,
I can look my dead friends in the face
As I couldn't two months ago.

War, The Liberator

Graduating in Arms

Mackintosh (seated, centre) with his officer cadet rowing team,
Cambridge 1917

The hospital in Earls Colne village hall where Sylvia worked

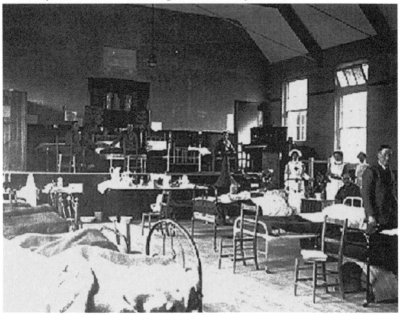

Shaun Thomas

CHAPTER 6
OUT OF ACTION
AUGUST 1916 – OCTOBER 1917

Oh, friends of mine, and I not there
To die along with you.

'Victory and Failure'
War, The Liberator

And so, abruptly, Alan Mackintosh returned from the comradeship of army life and the confusion of battle to the relative calm of home, and treatment. Despite having been wounded and gassed, his physical state did not prevent him attending to literary matters, since the final stages of the work that was to become his first anthology, *A Highland Regiment*, were in hand.

The contract with John Lane at the Bodley Head was signed by Mackintosh on 27th September 1916. The book was to retail at 3/6d, Mackintosh receiving royalties of 'ten percent (10%) of the published price of all copies sold (13 copies being reckoned as twelve), after the sale of five hundred copies (500) which shall be free of royalty'.

In Clause 15 Mackintosh agreed to 'purchase on day of publication one hundred copies of the said work at the published price.' It is clear that any financial risk in the publication was to be borne by the poet.[1]

By October he was stationed at Ripon in Yorkshire, with the 4th (Reserve) Battalion of the Seaforth Highlanders, a component of the 64th (Highland) Division, which trained replacements for the 51st Division in France. On October 25th Mackintosh wrote to John Lane in London, returning the typewritten poems for the book, with corrections.[2] On November 2nd he dealt with the

---

(1) The Bodley Head Collection, Reading University
(2) The Bodley Head Collection, Harry Ransom Humanities
    Research Center, University of Texas at Austin

question of asking publishers of his poems which had appeared in the English Review in June 1916 and Oxford Poetry 1914-1916, for their permission to reprint, and was keen to check that his dedication to the Regiment was going into the book. In this letter are indications that his convalescence was far from over, and that he is beginning to experience the frustration of relative inactivity:

> 'I'm still here with my leg pretty bad and one of my eyes almost blind; but it may not get any worse. I hope to be able to get up to town soon.'[3]

There is no direct evidence of his symptoms, but the effects of gas could include persistent and problematic secretions and blistering, and the destruction of enzymes which could lead to the progressive deterioration of the victim's sight. On November 7th[4] his mood had decidedly worsened:

> I'm still engaged in doing nothing in particular in this beastly hole, where, as you can see, there is not even black ink. It is a ghastly life and my eyes are possibly going blind which does not improve matters.

In this letter he was sending the corrected proofs to John Lane and sending additional poems to come at the end of 'the regimental part of the book'. It is probable that these were 'On Vimy Ridge' and 'In Memoriam (R.M. Stalker)'. In addition to containing specific memories of two recently fallen friends, Lt.William Reader, who had been mortally wounded on 30th July, and Lt. R.M. Stalker, formerly of the 5th Seaforths, who was declared 'missing' in September after transferring to the Royal Flying Corps, these poems deal extensively with Mackintosh's memories of the companionship of service life. The grief expressed is for the loss of this, as well as for his dead friends, whose fate weighed heavily on him, even more so since, as far as he knew at the time, both were missing in action:[5]

---

(3) HRHRC ibid

(4) HRHRC ibid

(5) Page 48 *A Highland Regiment* E.A. Mackintosh. John Lane, The Bodley Head, 1917

Oh, friends of mine, where are you now
Somewhere beneath the troubled sky,
With earth above a quiet brow,
Reader and Stalk for ever lie.

Strangely, whereas the Commonwealth War Graves Commission
records show that Stalker died on 8th September, Sutherland, in
the battalion history, says that Stalker transferred to the Royal Flying
Corps on 9th September: 'Lt. R.M. Stalker struck off strength on
joining the R.F.C.'

Mackintosh had been wounded on the same day as Reader,
and by the time of writing he was not aware that the latter had
been buried in the town cemetery at Dernancourt, near Albert.[6]

Both poems use the imagery of fire and ashes to denote life
and death, actual or emotional, and his use of both visual and aural
touches lifts these two poems above their uncomplicated form and
adds to the effect of the thoughts expressed. For instance, the second
stanza of 'On Vimy Ridge' sets the visual scene sharply, and makes
fire a metaphor for courage:[7]

And watched the fires of courage glow
Above the scattered ash of fear,
On Vimy Ridge four months ago.

The contrast of the glowing 'fires of courage' with 'scattered
ash of fear' is strong. In the last stanza of 'In Memoriam (R.M.
Stalker)' even the small substitute fire of the candle has burned
out: there is no colour, sound, warmth, or vigour. Mackintosh is
alone, and may have sat all night contemplating the loss of friends:

The candle's burned out now, old man,
And the dawn's come grey and cold,
And I sit by the fire here,
Alone and sad and old.

A reference to the Lairg clique elsewhere in this poem suggests
that some of the officers went there whilst training at Golspie in

(6) Commonwealth War Graves Commission
(7) *A Highland Regiment* ibid, page 48

1915, and that Mackintosh had made a reminiscent return to visit their old haunt, apparently on the day before he wrote the poem.

Whereas most of Mackintosh's war poems deal with personalities or single episodes, there is a notable exception, included near the end of *A Highland Regiment*. 'The Volunteer' spans the years 1914-1916, summing up his experience: he recognises his pre-combat immaturity and how he mentally attuned himself to be a warrior, mastering the mysteries of drill, relationships with all ranks, the acquisition of expertise with grenades, the leadership of men, and the control of fear, and concludes with the recognition that he cannot rekindle that innocence: front line experience has destroyed that ability and he is battle-worn, devoid of enthusiasm:[8]

> I took my heart from the fire of love,
> Molten and warm not yet shaped clear,
> And tempered it to steel of proof
> Upon the anvil block of fear. . .
>
> But as the heavy days went on
> The fire that once had warmed it grew
> Duller, and presently was gone. . .
>
> Dead embers of a greying fire.
> I cannot melt my heart again.

It is hard to reconcile the Mackintosh of this period, physically and emotionally traumatised as he evidently was, with the soldier returning to France the following year. The adequacy of his recovery by that time must remain in some doubt.

Home again, with no immediate prospect of serving overseas, he further reflected on the previous years and in 'Recruiting'[9] (see page 139) highlighted the gap that separated blood-thirsty armchair civilian strategists from the front line soldiers. By the time he wrote this poem conscription had been introduced, as the well of volunteers that had supplied the army with its recruits had almost run dry. He scorns shallow patriotism, and condemns the women

---

(8) *A Highland Regiment* ibid, page 47

(9) Page 15 *War, The Liberator* E.A.Mackintosh. John Lane, The
    Bodley Head, 1918

who, early in the war, gave white feathers to men who were not in uniform:

Help to keep them nice and safe
From the wicked German foe,
Don't let him come over here!
'Lads, you're wanted – out you go.'

The second half of the poem then contrasts with this, by encouraging youngsters to join:

Better twenty honest years
Than their dull three score and ten.
Lads, you're wanted. Come and learn
To live and die with honest men.

It expresses a serving soldier's view of the unreality of civilian attitudes to the war, of his belief that the Western Front was the world's crucible, of the debt that he believed was owed to the dead, that he could write this. A modern analogy might be that of someone who is devoted to the developing world, where individuals' choices are few, being irritated on their return to Western Europe with its rampant consumerism.

Mackintosh sent a telegram from Ripon to John Lane on November 9th[10] to confirm that he had returned the corrected proofs of *A Highland Regiment*. On November 10th 1916 the *John O'Groat Journal* reported that Mackintosh, on a recent visit to Wick, mentioned being 'very pleased with the part the North boys played in the raid which brought him his cross.'[11] He had travelled North to see Captain Milligan, who had been invalided out of the 5th Seaforths. He may also have visited Sinclair Sutherland, David Sutherland's father, who was a widower, and possibly Stalker's parents, Charlotte and George, who lived at Wick. The trip to Lairg is likely to have been part of the same Scottish journey. For this to have been 'recent', in the terms of the *John O' Groat Journal* item, but to have pre-dated the writing of 'In Memoriam (R.M.Stalker)' sent off to London on November 7th, it must have occurred in

(10) HRHRC, ibid

(11) *John O' Groat Journal* Nov.10, 1916

October, perhaps whilst he was on leave from the Reserve Battalion at Ripon, or even before he joined it.

In mid-November Mackintosh received the news of the 5th Seaforths involvement in the 51st (Highland) Division's attack on Beaumont Hamel, during the last phase of the Somme battle. The battalion occupied a position on the Auchonvillers-Beaumont Hamel road, and their objective when the attack began on 13th November was a German trench two hundred yards east of the latter village. Machine-gun fire and uncut wire inhibited their advance, with fog making progress even more difficult. By the end of the day the division had established a line on the eastern edge of the village: the 5th Seaforths had used bombing parties to good effect during the battle. At the end of the day the battalion was temporarily down to 90 men, but it stayed in the line until the night of 14th/ 15th November, repelling counter-attacks. A party led by Lt. A.J. MacKay reconnoitred and took sixty prisoners. From the 19th the battalion was again defending the line. When they were relieved on the 24th the toll of casualties was 94 killed or died of wounds, 193 wounded and 5 missing.[12]

Having moved down from Ripon to Downing College in Cambridge to prepare for his new posting with No.2 Officer Cadet Battalion, Mackintosh wrote to John Lane, on 1st December[13] saying that he was 'very braced just now' due to his regiment's capture of Beaumont Hamel, and replying to Lane's request for an opinion of the manuscript of 'Pip Squeak and Others', the story of an Irish New Army (Kitchener volunteer) battalion, which Mackintosh criticised both for length and content. Lane was utilising Mackintosh's first hand experience, taking advantage of the fact that *A Highland Regiment* was finished, and had possibly been trying to distract him from the boredom he felt at Ripon.

The many poems that Mackintosh wrote concerning the fighting at Beaumont Hamel show that it had an immediate and lasting impact on him, the dating of some of the pieces indicating that he must have begun them fairly soon after the event. He responded to his comrades' military success, but did not shrink from addressing the horror of the slaughter involved. In 'Beaumont Hamel – Captured

---

(12) Page 101 *War Diary of the 5th Seaforth Highlanders*, Capt. D.Sutherland. John Lane, 1920

(13) HRHRC, ibid

November 16th, 1916' (the battle ended on the 16th, having begun
on the 13th; Mackintosh's date may be based on a press account),
he writes of the dead who lay in the harsh November surroundings,
which could no longer affect them:[14]

> You that were so warm once,
> Flesh and blood and brain,
> You've made an end of dying,
> Hurts and cold and crying,
> And all but quiet lying,
> Easeful after pain.

He reflects that they may return in the night, as fierce ghosts,
though the spur to his personal memories is that of joyful musical
sessions now reduced in his mind to the echo of bagpipe laments
on the battlefield. He acknowledges a broader memory: that of the
nation from which the dead men came:

> And all our children dreaming
> Shall see your bayonets gleaming,
> Scotland's warriors streaming
> Forward evermore.

It is an illustration based on his background and culture: the
imagery is redundant now.

In another poem, 'From Home – To the men who fell at
Beaumont Hamel, November 13th 1916' Mackintosh painfully
contrasts his own remote, removed situation, and regrets not being
with his comrades: the feeling of isolation from his battalion was
experienced by many:[15]

> The veil is rent with a rifle flash
> And shows me plain to see
> Battle and bodies of men that lived
> And fought along with me.
> Oh, God! it would not have been so hard
> If I'd been in it too.

---

(14) *War, The Liberator* ibid, page 20

(15) *War, The Liberator* ibid, page 29

KILTS AND KILLING.

The seeds of his wish to return are obvious, even as he threw himself into his work with No.2 Officer Cadet Battalion. His role was to impart his expertise in bombing techniques, but he took an interest in the cadets' rowing activities, and when Spring came would train the eight they had formed, trying to give the cadets a flavour of pre-war university life. The souvenir magazine, 'Graduating-in-Arms' thanked him for his participation, and included a head and shoulders caricature of him, surrounded by exploding missiles.[16]

On January 11th 1917 Mackintosh wrote to John Lane to ask when *A Highland Regiment* would be published. His mother had sent a cheque to the publisher, covering the cost of Mackintosh's contracted one hundred personal copies:[17]

> When will the book be coming out? I understand there ought to be a decent sale in the North. Isn't this damnable weather? My leg's giving me the jumps these days.

At that time he felt able to rise above his persistent physical symptoms, though the work was obviously strenuous and exacting, since by 27th January[18] he was writing to John Lane:

> I am sorry not to have written before but I'm so overworked now that I get too tired to remember.

This is confirmed by the course booklet, which describes him as an 'energetic bombing specialist' and remarks that the instructors showed 'readiness to give advice and instruction not only during parade hours but also in their own very limited spare time.'

---

(16) K.F.Kidson in 'Graduating-in-arms', souvenir magazine of No.2 Officer Cadet Battalion, Cambridge, Dec.1916-May 1917

(17) HRHRC, ibid

(18) HRHRC, ibid

After the publication of *A Highland Regiment* in January 1917 Mackintosh mentioned in the January 27th letter that 'the dons are booming me quite nicely', an indication of the congratulations he was receiving from his hosts. On February 11th he wrote again to order twenty copies of the book,[19] but this time from Brighton, where he was staying with members of his family. Though a trip home to celebrate the publication is quite conceivable, his remark about worsening health raises the question of whether he was too ill to remain on duty:

> Isn't the weather rotten? I'm a cripple again so I
> suppose I've seen the last of this war.

He must have been heartened by the encouraging reviews which *A Highland Regiment* was attracting, which are interesting examples of contemporary reactions to the book:[20]

> . . . nearly half the poems in his *A Highland Regiment* were
> written in the days of peace. Hence this is an unusually
> interesting volume; it enables the student of poetry to
> examine in the work of one man what the influence of
> war has been on the poetic spirit. Briefly, it may be said
> that a comparison between the peace and war verse of
> Mr. Mackintosh shows that the latter is superior to the
> former, and that the native Celtic temperament of the
> writer has been greatly intensified by his experience of
> the clash of arms.   (*The Daily Graphic*)

> . . . he cultivated the muses in the classical shades of Isis
> before the war gave a keener edge to his thoughts and to
> his verse. The pieces written during his training and in
> the trenches are of no ordinary quality, for they have the
> haunting melody which is the peculiar gift of the Gaelic
> temperament.   (*The Globe*)

> His poems from the war, and even those written on the
> way to it, reveal him as a true poet, both born and made,

---

(19) HRHRC, ibid
(20) Reviews quoted on advertising pages in *War, The Liberator*

> with a style purged of all its former cleverness and
> insincerity. (*Morning Post*)

The distinction these critics make directly or by implication between Mackintosh's pre-war poems and his war poems is easily understood.

On February 18th he wrote from Cambridge to a Mr. Willett at the Bodley Head. He was already bringing together trench songs, which were to appear later in *War, The Liberator*. They were apparently intended for separate publication at a later stage:[21]

> I enclose the collection of trench songs. I'm afraid I've
> had to cut out a few of the best and some of those I've
> left in are pretty fragmentary. Still if you think it's worth
> publishing, I should say it could be at all events as
> amusing as most similar publications and a great deal
> truer. There are of course a good many local allusions
> but they cannot be cut out without spoiling the songs.

After that date no further correspondence is to hand, and, therefore, no evidence of early plans for a second anthology, or indeed, how much, if anything, had been decided about this before Mackintosh's return to France and his subsequent death in action.

Mackintosh undoubtedly found much pleasure in composing and performing parodies and songs for the cadets on the course as he had experienced behind the lines in France. This is made clear in 'The Baleful Bard – or the Muse Munition Making':[22]

> And now sequestered in this quiet nook,
> I struggle to instruct the wise cadet
> In bombing, (not according to the book)
> Patrols and how most surely to revet
> The crumbling trenches on the local hill,
> And oft to the jocund piano's strain
> I mount upon the platform with a will
> To sing these ancient songs of mine again. . .

---

(21) HRHRC, ibid

(22) *War, The Liberator* ibid, page 85

The parody 'Sniper Sandy' immortalised Sergeant Alexander MacDonald who would have been in Mackintosh's thoughts since he had been killed with the 5th Seaforths at Beaumont Hamel. It may well have been included in the batch sent earlier to Mr. Willett. Though apparently written at an earlier time, when it was later published in *War, The Liberator* a post Beaumont Hamel dedication is included. Sung to the tune of 'Sister Susie's Sewing Shirts for Soldiers', the parody expresses attitudes that, even then, might have been unacceptable outside the context of a soldiers' sing-song:[23]

Chorus –
Sniper Sandy's slaying Saxon soldiers
And Saxon soldiers seldom show but Sandy slays a few,
And every day the Bosches put up little wooden crosses
In the cemetery for Saxon soldiers Sandy slew.

Another song, 'To Basil, A Bavarian Bomber – In Memory of the Barricades in the Labyrinth',[24] returns more humorously to Mackintosh's experience of the previous Spring, and his attitude to the enemy is the same as that expressed in 'Snow in France' (see Chapter 3):

Often men came to me and said that they
Had done you in at last and heard you yell,
But 'twas my sorrow on th'ensuing day
To hear again the voice I knew so well.

The trenches in the Labyrinth had been closer than fifty yards from one another, and soldiers often exchanged pleasantries and insults across No Man's Land. It is conceivable that Mackintosh and his men could identify a specific individual's voice. Despite the fact that they had been trying to kill one another, there was no real malice, indeed there is almost affection, in Mackintosh's imagined meeting with Basil after the war:

And we shall meet, oh peerless grenadier –

---

(23) *War, The Liberator* ibid, page 114
(24) *War, The Liberator* ibid, page 93

> Impotent things my poor old Millses were,
> My punch is not a dud, I promise you.

According to John Murray's 'Memoir' Mackintosh fell in love while he was at Cambridge, became engaged, and planned to emigrate to New Zealand after the war with his fiancée.[25]

It is not known exactly where or when he met Sylvia Marsh, although it is most likely they met 1917 – the fact that his one poem to her was written after his return to France in the autumn of that year suggests that the romance blossomed through the Spring and summer. Her identity is in a letter that Mackintosh sent to his sister Muriel.[26] His fiancée was Edith Sylvia Marsh, born on 14th July 1890 in Surrey to Edith and Charles Henry Marsh.[27]

Sylvia worked as a nursing member of the Voluntary Aid Detachment, at Earls Colne Red Cross Hospital, Essex, from September 1915 until December 1917. The hospital had been established in the village hall with 12 beds, rising in 1915 to 35 beds.[28] Earls Colne was then linked to Cambridge by an hour and a half's journey on the Colne Valley Light Railway – whether they were introduced at a social occasion, or met by chance in Cambridge, is not known. Sylvia was later described in her marriage certificate in 1922 as a masseuse, so it is possible that he met her when he was having treatment for his leg.

His dedicatory poem 'To Sylvia' which begins *War, The Liberator*, and was written in France on 20th October 1917, refers to a time when they were together in August. Wherever they met, and when, the poem typifies the closeness of an engaged couple, as does the plan to emigrate to New Zealand. There was some measure of agreement between Mackintosh and his fiancée on matters of importance, since Murray states that Mackintosh had much in common with her ideals and principles.[29] Sylvia Marsh was a Quaker who would have a well-developed social conscience, and Mackintosh's Fabian principles would be akin to many of these. Whatever

---

(25) 'Memoir' in *War, The Liberator* ibid, page 3

(26) Last letter from Mackintosh to Muriel and Sylvia. Rosemary Beazley

(27) Quakers Friends Library Birth Records. Julian Duffus

(28) Letter from British Red Cross to Julian Duffus, 1995

(29) 'Memoir', ibid, page 4

romantic attraction they had for one another would have been enhanced by their similar views of the world.

By the end of April 1917, Alan Mackintosh's wish to return to active service was becoming much stronger. This is evident in his 'Three Battles' cycle of poems dedicated to the 51st (Highland) Division. After featuring the High Wood and Beaumont Hamel campaigns, 'Three Battles' culminates in a poem entitled 'Victory and Failure' concerning the grim determination shown at Arras and Roeux that year. He deeply regrets that he is far away from his division:[30]

I think I see again
The bodies of my friends that lie
Unburied in the dew –
Oh, friends of mine, and I not there
To die along with you.

Captain Sutherland vividly described the conditions of the battlefield during the fighting of 9th April,[31] on the right flank of the famous Canadian capture of Vimy Ridge. Advancing from trenches in their old sector near Vimy, the 5th Seaforths eventually took three German trench systems:

It was a bitterly cold morning with a strong wind and heavy rain showers, changing into snow later on. Line after line of enemy trenches were taken, although the Bavarians on our front, the finest fighting material in the German army, fought stubbornly, some groups fighting on until every men was killed.

On 23rd April the battalion took part in the attack on the Chemical Works at Roeux, east of Arras. This was a well-defended German strongpoint made up of cellars, dug-outs and machine-gun emplacements. It is quite possible that Mackintosh received, from Sutherland, descriptions of the events similar to those in the battalion history. Sutherland related that the soldiers had rushed through the German fortress:[32]

---

(30) *War, The Liberator* ibid, page 28

(31) Sutherland, ibid, page 100

(32) Sutherland, ibid, page 109-110

... and quickly had it in their hands. Then came a
tremendous counter-attack, strongly supported by heavy
artillery fire, and our men were forced to withdraw.
Rallied, they came on again and drove the Bosche out.

Mackintosh's sense of guilt that he was not involved was to
increase. He had acknowledged in a lighter vein, in 'The Baleful
Bard', that he would eventually return:[33]

But lo, there comes a yet more dreadful day,
When with his pleasant months of Blighty o'er
The bard shall lift his pack and hie away
To land again upon the Gallic shore. . .

Decision is hauntingly specific in 'From Home – Cambridge'
which contrasts the comforts of home and prospects of a bright
future as an up-and-coming poet, with the war to which Mackintosh
feels inexorably drawn, and in which he had already won honour
with the award of the Military Cross.[34] The poem raises the question
of whether he was thinking metaphorically of his 'dead friends. . .
calling' in the penultimate line, or whether he was literally waking
in the night, haunted in his dreams by his dead friends or seeing
them in day-time flashbacks:

Here there is peace and comfort for me,
A warm soft bed and a good roof o'er me,
Here maybe there is fame before me,
Honour and fame for all I know,

Back to the trench that I see so clearly,
Back to the fight I can see so nearly,

Dear friends of mine, oh, cease your calling,
For I come back to you.

In late September 1917 Mackintosh left for France, drawn to
his fate by a combination of patriotism, loyalty to his battalion, and

(33) *War, The Liberator* ibid, page 85
(34) *War, The Liberator* ibid, page 31

guilt at his survival, the last nowadays recognised as a characteristic symptom of post traumatic stress syndrome. He told his sister Muriel 'I've got to get back to my Jocks'.[35] It is probable that his determination to return had grown throughout late 1916 and 1917, and had preceded his relationship with Sylvia.

It is unlikely that he was fully fit for front line service. Although his leg may have improved, the blast or gas-induced deterioration of his eyesight would be continuing. It is easy to imagine him persuading a malleable Medical Officer to pass him as fit, especially in the wake of the Third Battle of Ypres, better known as Passchendaele, which had sorely depleted the army in France in August.

The pain of parting from his fiancée is expressed in 'To Sylvia'.[36] Being a Quaker, Sylvia was a pacifist. She worked in a hospital and would know how unfit he was, having seen the effects of permanently incapacitating wounds. Her distress that he was choosing to leave her of his own volition to put himself back into danger is easy to imagine. Sylvia would have been aware that fitter young men were managing to remain at home with less serious medical conditions, or in non-combatant postings. If his love for her was all that he had undoubtedly proclaimed it to be, it would be incomprehensible to her that he could leave her because of a burden of guilt owed to his living and dead comrades. She must have feared for his life, knowing that subalterns led from the front and suffered disproportionately high casualties. Both her emotion and her logic would suggest that he should be satisfied with a full year's service on the Western Front, an M.C. and a wound, a conclusion probably endorsed by most of her friends and his relatives. She would be afraid that her new-found love, with all the promise of a bright future together in New Zealand, was being put at unnecessary risk.

It is clear from the poem that he had shared his tortured guilt at being safe and alive with her, and that she had not understood, and had been deeply upset, to the extent that he suggests that she would eventually forgive him. Yet there is a calm assurance in the last two lines that indicate that, whatever his regrets about leaving Sylvia, he was at peace with himself in a way that he had not been at Cambridge:

---

(35) Family information: Rosemary Beazley

(36) Frontispiece poem, *War*, *The Liberator*

But you'll forgive me yet, my dear,
Because of what you know,
I can look my dead friends in the face
As I couldn't two months ago.

FAREWELL TO SERGEANT H. FRASER AND L.-SERGEANT G.M'KAY

Well, you have gone now, comrades,
And we shall see no more
The gallant friendly faces
Framed in my dug-out door.
I had no words to tell you
The things I longed to say,
But the company is empty
Since you have gone away.

The company is filled now
With faces strange to see,
And scarce a man of the old men
That lived and fought with me.
I know the drafts are good men,
I know they're doing well,
But they're not the men I slept with
Those nights at La Boiselle.

Oh, the old days of friendship
We shall not see again,
The bitter winter trenches
And the marches in the rain.
Bécourt, Authuille, Thiepval,
Henancourt, Avelay,
Their names are keys that open
Remembered doors to me.

Doors that will open never
Upon this tortured land.
I shall not see you ever,
Or take you by the hand.
Only for ancient friendship,
For all the times we knew,
Maybe you will remember
As I remember you.

War, The Liberator

GHOSTS OF WAR
(SENT FROM FRANCE IN OCTOBER 1917)

When you and I are buried
With grasses over head,
The memory of our fights will stand
Above this bare and tortured land,
We knew ere we were dead.

Though grasses grow at Vimy,
And poppies at Messines,
And in High Wood the children play,
The craters and the graves will stay
To show what things have been.

Though all be quiet in day-time,
The night shall bring a change,
And peasants walking home will see
Shell-torn meadow and riven tree,
And their own fields grown strange.

They shall hear live men crying,
They shall see dead men lie,
Shall hear the rattling Maxims fire,
And by the broken twists of wire
Gold flares light up the sky.

And in their new-built houses
The frightened folk will see
Pale bombers coming down the street,
And hear the flurry of charging feet,
And the crash of Victory.

This is our Earth baptizèd
With the red wine of War.
Horror and courage hand in hand
Shall brood upon the stricken land
In silence evermore.

War, The Liberator

MINES
(SENT FROM FRANCE IN NOVEMBER 1917)

What are you doing, Sentry,
Fresh-faced and brown?
Waiting for the mines, Sir,
Sitting on the mines, Sir,
Just to keep them down.
Mines going up, and no one to tell for us
Where it will be, and may be it's as well for us,
Mines, going up. Oh, God, but it's hell for us,
Here with the bloody mines.

What are you doing, Sentry,
Cold and drawn and grey?
Listening to them tap, Sir,
Same old tap, tap, tap, Sir
And praying for the day.
Mines going up, and no one can say for us
When it will be; but they are waiting some day for us,
Mines going up – oh! Folk at home pray for us
Here with the bloody mines.

Where are you lying, Sentry?
Wasn't this your place?
Down below your feet, Sir,
Below your heavy feet, Sir,
With earth upon my face.
Mines going up, and the earth and the clod on us –
Fighting for breath – and our own comrades trod on us.
Mines going up – Have pity, oh God! on us,
Down in the bloody mines.

War, The Liberator

DEATH

Because I have made light of death
And mocked at wounds and pain,
The doom is laid on me to die –
Like the humble men in days gone by –
That angered me to hear them cry
For pity to me in vain.

I shall not go out suddenly
As many a man has done.
But I shall lie as those men lay –
Longing for death the whole long day –
Praying, as I heard those men pray,
And none shall heed me, none.

The fierce waves will go surging on
Before they tend to me.
Oh, God of battles, I pray you send
No word of pity-no help no friend,
That if my spirit break at the end
None may be there to see.

War, The Liberator

WAR, THE LIBERATOR
(TO THE AUTHORESS OF 'NON-COMBATANTS')

Surely War is vile to you, you who can but know of it,
Broken men and broken hearts, and boys too young to die,
You that never knew its joy, never felt the glow of it,
Valour and the pride of men. soaring to the sky.
Death's a fearful thing to you, terrible in suddenness,
Lips that will not laugh again, tongues that will not sing,
You that have not ever seen their sudden life of happiness,
The moment they looked on death, a cowed and beaten thing.

Say what life would theirs have been, that it should make you
                  weep for them,
A small grey world imprisoning the wings of their desire?
Happier than they could tell who knew not life would
                  keep for them
Fragments of high Romance, the old Heroic fire.
All they dreamed of childishly, bravery and fame for them,
Charges at the cannon's mouth, enemies they slew,
Bright across the waking world their romances came for them,
Is not life a little price when our dreams come true?

All the terrors of the night, doubts and thoughts tormenting us,
Boy-minds painting quiveringly the awful face of fear,
These are gone for ever now, truth is come contenting us,
Night with all its tricks is gone and our eyes are clear.
Now in all the time to come, memory will cover us,
Trenches that we did not lose, charges that we made,
Since a voice, when first we heard the shells go shrilling over us,
Said within us, 'This is Death – and I am not afraid!'

Since we felt our spirits tower, smiling and contemptuous,
O'er the little frightened things, running to and fro,
Looked on Death and saw a slave blustering and presumptuous,
Daring vainly still to bring Man his master low.
Though we knew that at the last, he would have his lust of us,
Carelessly we braved his might, felt and knew not why
Something stronger than ourselves, moving in the dust of us,
Something in the Soul of Man still too great to die.

War, The Liberator

A CREED

Out of the womb of time and dust of the years forgotten,
   Spirit and fire enclosed in mutable flesh and bone,
Came down a road unknown the thing that is me for ever,
   The lonely soul of a man that stands by itself alone.

This is the right of my race, the heritage won by my fathers,
   Theirs by the years of fighting, theirs by the price they paid,
Making a son like them, careless of hell of heaven,
   A man that can look in the face of the gods and be not afraid.

Poor and weak is my strength and I cannot war against heaven,
   Strong, too strong are the gods; but there is one thing that I can
Claim like a man unashamed, the full reward of my virtues,
   Pay like a man the price for the sins I sinned as a man.

Now is the time of trial, the end of the years of fighting,
   And the echoing gates roll back on the country I cannot see,
If it be life that waits I shall live for ever unconquered,
   If death I shall die at last strong in my pride and free.

Vimy Ridge, 1916
A Highland Regiment

Rosemary Beazley

Lieutenant E. Alan Mackintosh, MC
before his return to France, 1917

Germans fortifying Cantaing Mill shortly before the battle

R. and C. Lesniak

CHAPTER 7

RETURN TO THE FRONT

The memory of our fights will stand
Above this bare and tortured land
We knew ere we were dead.

'Ghosts of War' *War, The Liberator*

By the time Alan Mackintosh had returned to France he had lost yet another friend to the ravages of war. Edmund Solomon, who had become a 2nd Lieutenant in the 1st South Lancashire Regiment, was killed in action on 2nd August 1917 at the age of 23. He was attached to the 8th Battalion which took part in relieving the 2nd Devons on Windhoek Ridge, and on a relatively quiet day, while he was visiting his machine-gun posts, he was hit in the stomach and died.[1]

In 'Memoir' John Murray says that Mackintosh's prose piece 'Gold Braid'[2] in *War, The Liberator* commemorated Solomon. This intriguing account of a visit to the site of a comrade's death is a composite of different stories and personalities, and appears to contain more fictional elements than the other two 'studies in war psychology'. It is evident, however, that Mackintosh wished he had been serving with Solomon at the time of his death, and had wanted to visit the place where his friend was killed. Mackintosh once again assumes the name of 'Tagg', MacTaggart, but with the higher rank of captain, and 'Lieutenant Andrew Mackay' (Solomon, if John Murray was correct) is said to have been a member of the '1st Sutherland Highlanders'. A sergeant guiding Tagg during his visit is the cause of some irritation:

---

(1) Capt W. Whalley-Kelley, *'Ich Dien' The South Lancashire Regiment 1914-1918* pub.1938

(2) *War, The Liberator* E.A.Mackintosh. John Lane, The Bodley Head, 1918

'I think this is the place, Sirr,' said the Sergeant, glaring
through his periscope at the German trench sixty yards
away. 'It was on the parapet yonder – that he died, Sirr –
was it not . . .' perhaps it was that fear and reverence of
death that irritated; he had never been afraid of death –
nor had old Andy.[3]

The officer grieves, though he knows that his friend had cared
little about the usual rites of passage:

The men lowered the wooden cross till the position met
with their officer's approval. He watched it sombrely –
that little cross was all they had to show for Andy; that
and memory. It was a good thing that Andy didn't care
about being buried properly and death and hell and all
that rot.[4]

In fact, the circumstances of Solomon's death meant that he
does have a grave, in Belgium, in Battery Corner Cemetery, near
Ypres.[5] Mackintosh seems to be reliving the emotional pain of the
raid in the Labyrinth (see Chapter 4) and combining circumstances
of that raid with the mourning of his close friend who died far
away from him:[6]

Andy had died on the Bosche parapet and he'd had the
wounded to bring in, and that was the end of it all. He
would never see Andy again. . .

He temporarily betrays a desire for his own life to end:

What a bloody war it was. What was the sense of it all? And
he used to think war was good fun – but then Andy had

---

(3) *War, The Liberator* ibid, page 153

(4) *War, The Liberator* ibid, page 154

(5) Plot 1, Row J, Grave 14 (Commonwealth War Graves
   Commission, Enquiries Department)

(6) *War, The Liberator* ibid, page 155

(7) *War, The Liberator* ibid, page 155

been there to enjoy it with him. Why couldn't he die too?[7]

Then, at the end of the unfinished piece, self preservation reasserts itself as a missile comes over:

> Gone was the mourner longing for death and peace; in
> his place was a wary animal, alert and fearful, watching
> the bomb with rapid and instinctive calculation.[8]

From the time he returned to France Mackintosh increasingly foretold his own death in poetry. 'Ship of the Soul', dedicated to Solomon, may have been written before going back, but is part of this process. Likening himself and his friend to Egyptian voyagers of ancient times, and to all 'souls' who still venture out, Mackintosh secs no possibility of a return home such as others will have. The two voyagers will be prisoners in a final limbo:

> Others may find their loves and keep them,
> But for us two there still shall be
> A kinder heart and a fairer city,
> The home and wife we shall never see.
> Lost adventurers watching ever
> Over the toss of the tricksy foam,
> Many a joyous port and city,
> Never the harbour lights of home.[9]

These stanzas evoke Mackintosh's parting from his fiancée and his fear that they will not be reunited. Mackintosh did not return to his former battalion, the 5th Seaforths: the war diary of the 4th (Ross Highland) Battalion Seaforths records on 3rd October 1917:[10]

> Warm day. Coys. At musketry. Physical training etc. Lt.C.
> (*sic*) A. Mackintosh, 2nd. Lts Gander, H.Paterson and
> E.J.Martin joined the battalion.

---

(8) *War, The Liberator* ibid, page 156

(9) *War, The Liberator* ibid, page 35

(10) 4th Seaforths' battalion war diary. Queen's Own Highlanders Museum, Inverness

The battalion was at Courcelles-le-Comte, near Bapaume.[11] Mackintosh's arrival in the 4th Battalion rather than rejoining his comrades in the 5th, may have been dictated by a greater need for replacement officers due to losses in 3rd Ypres, or he may have requested a posting to the 4th since his university friend Andrew Fraser was one of the battalion's officers. The battalion went into the front line between Vis-en-Artois and Guemappe from 5th to 12th/13th October, then recommenced training. During this period the battalion was billeted in shelters near Marlières Caves and at Carlisle Huts near the Arras-Bapaume road. Before the next tour of duty in the front line on 21st October, Mackintosh had written 'To Sylvia'.

Two other poems have connections with this general period, and may have been written during this same training time, or later in the month when the battalion was in rest billets. 'Farewell' is a moving tribute to two comrades who were in the Somme area in 1915 with Mackintosh. As with 'In Memoriam', he is saluting specific named men who were not officers, in this case 'Sergeant H.Fraser and L.Sergeant G.M'Kay'. This makes Mackintosh rare among poets of the First World War. In the poem he contrasts the early days of companionship with a changed situation, surrounded by unfamiliar faces:

> Well, you have gone now, comrades,
> And I shall see no more
> The gallant friendly faces
> Framed in my dug-out door. . .
>
> I shall not see you ever,
> Or take you by the hand.
> Only for ancient friendship,
> For all the times we knew,
> Maybe you will remember
> As I remember you.[12]

Though the poem applies to the time when Mackintosh was serving with the 5th Seaforths, and is placed in *War, The Liberator*

---

(11) *A History of the 4th Bn. Seaforth Highlanders*
Lt.Col.M.Haldane. Witherby, 1928

(12) *War, The Liberator* ibid, page 23

before the group of poems relating to the action at Beaumont Hamel in 1916, there are no comrades of the names in the dedication who were killed while in the Somme area. They had served with him on the Somme and in the Labyrinth. Who were they?

Lance Sergeant George McKay of the 5th Seaforths came from Dorrery, Calder, Thurso and was the eldest son of the late William MacKay and Mrs MacKay.[13] His name is on the Halkirk War Memorial and he is buried in Highland Cemetery, Roclincourt.[14] He was killed at Arras on 9th April 1917, a battle featured by Mackintosh in his 'Three Battles' poem sequence.[15] He is the most likely candidate for 'L.Sergeant G. M'Kay' known by Mackintosh the year before.

No possible N.C.O. with the surname Fraser fits the circumstances. Hubert Heron Fraser, a temporary 2nd Lieutenant attached to the 8th Seaforths, 15th (Scottish) Division, was wounded on 22nd August 1917 in an attack on German pillboxes at Beck House and Iberian Farm in the Steenbeke area, near Ypres, and died of his wounds in France on 18th October.[16] He is buried at Étaples Cemetery,[17] and was the son of the Rev. James and Mrs Elizabeth Fraser of 1 Eskbank Terrace, Dalkeith.

Mackintosh may have learned of Fraser's death through newspapers, or from fellow soldiers, since the 15th (Scottish) Division was stationed around Arras in the autumn of 1917. If Fraser had been promoted from the ranks and his previous battalion had been the 5th Seaforths, he could have been the Fraser in the poem's dedication. Mackintosh would then have written the poem in France in October or early November 1917 once he had heard of Fraser's death, and while missing the companionship evoked in the poem. There were many faces 'strange to see' around him at this time.

The poem 'Ghosts of War'[18] has the note 'sent from France in

---

(13) Caithness War Records, 1914-1918. Ally Budge

(14) Plot 2, Row A, Grave 47 (Commonwealth War Graves Commission, Enquiries Department)

(15) *War, The Liberator* ibid, page 25

(16) Commonwealth War Graves Commission Casualty Search Results

(17) Plot 28, Row B, Grave 8 (Commonwealth War Graves Commission, Enquiries Department)

(18) *War, The Liberator* ibid, page 38

October 1917' beneath its title in *War, The Liberator*. Mackintosh is speaking of a time after his own death:

> When you and I are buried
> With grasses over head,
> The memory of our fights will stand
> Above this bare and tortured land,
> We knew ere we were dead.

Who is the 'you' in this? Though probably referring to fellow soldiers in general, Mackintosh writes in a personal way that is not unlike that seen in his poems with a specific dedication. He goes on to picture villagers returning after the war being haunted by those who fought:

> And in their new built houses,
> The frightened folk will see
> Pale bombers coming down the street,
> And hear the flurry of charging feet,
> And the crash of victory.

With the mention of bombers Mackintosh numbers himself among the ghosts. The final stanza mingles religious ceremony with the spilling of soldiers' blood to show how the land will be ineradicably affected by all that has happened there:

> This is our earth baptizèd
> With the red wine of War.

Mackintosh was wrong about one aspect of the countryside's future: in an earlier stanza he mentions that children will once again play in High Wood. This is, of course, impossible to the present day, due to buried unexploded shells, and the land therefore still has physical scars which he did not envisage.

On October 28th the battalion was in rest billets in Izel-les-Hameaux,[19] quite near their old billets in the Labyrinth sector. Here Mackintosh's close friend Andy Fraser rejoined the battalion, along with several officers and men. According to Haldane, this proved

---

(19) 4th Seaforths' battalion war diary, ibid

to be: 'one of the pleasantest rest billets that the Battalion had occupied.'[20] There was time for training, sports, and commemoration of the Divisional involvement at Beaumont a year before. Mackintosh would have had the opportunity at Izel-les-Hameaux to work on his poetry; perhaps he also visited the graves of those killed in the raid in May 1916.

This last period of rest is when the poem 'Mines' was written, since it was annotated 'sent from France in November 1917' and recalls, according to Captain David Sutherland[21] the time when the 5th Seaforths had been in the line near Bécourt in early 1916, although it may refer to the frequent mining in the Labyrinth. Mackintosh captures the misery of the sentry knowing that the Germans are tunnelling under him, preparatory to blowing up his trench. Although the front line numbers were reduced when a mine was imminent, individuals had to remain there to guard it against conventional raids. This was probably worse than the unannounced detonation of a mine. In either case, the results were disastrous for the people involved – death, dismemberment and suffocation, followed by a determined enemy infantry attack.

Mackintosh deals in 'Mines' with the whole of a soldier's experience from danger through fear, to death, and adds a hitherto-absent detailed realism which indicates an ability to write in a less intensely personal way. While he has frequently dealt with the broad subject of death this is the first time he has, while writing about the fate of the sentry, approached an illustration of the awfulness of war in the same vein as the work of Owen and Sassoon:

> Where are you lying, Sentry?
> Wasn't this your place?
> Down below your feet, Sir,
> Below your heavy feet, Sir,
> With earth upon my face.
> Mines going up, and the earth and the clod on us –
> Fighting for breath – and our own comrades trod on us.[22]

---

(20) Haldane, ibid., page 239

(21) Page 37 War Diary of the 5th Seaforth Highlanders
Capt.D.Sutherland. John Lane, 1920

(22) *War, The Liberator* ibid, page 40

That Mackintosh was still preoccupied by thoughts of his men who died in the raid is evident in the short poem 'Death' which features the fairly imminent prospect, for him, of his own demise. He critically derides himself for having 'mocked at wounds and pain' and treated death too lightly, now foreseeing a slow death in the heat of battle, with the possibility of his courage failing: battle fields were littered with uncollected wounded, often for days, some dying slowly and noisily:

> Oh, God of battles I pray you send
> No word of pity – no help, no friend,
> That if my spirit break at the end
> None may be there to see.[23]

On 16th November, the last day of the rest period, there was a final performance of the battalion Officers' Concert Party, an occasion at which it would have been natural to find Mackintosh taking part. Haldane remarks in his battalion history that: '. . . few, alas, of the performers were left when the Battalion next came out to rest. It was a most amusing performance, for the Party was a good one.'[24]

The battalion left at 10p.m. that night, and marched to Beaumetz where it entrained. By the 19th it was billeted in the ruined village of Metz, where the troops waited to take part in the attack on the Hindenburg line the following day. Here he wrote his last letter to Sylvia and to his sister Muriel,[25] folding it and addressing it to both of them. The message was terse:

> 4th Seaforth 19/11/17
> My darling Muriel/girl (one overwritten on the other)
> We're going over tomorrow so I'm leaving this in case I don't come back. Goodbye. No time for more.
>
> Your loving
> Alan

---

(23) *War, The Liberator* ibid, page 42

(24) Haldane, ibid, page 239

(25) Letter in possession of Rosemary Beazley

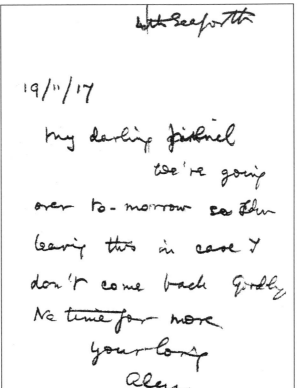

A hasty note on a fragment of paper: not the kind of prepared epistle carefully composed by others for their surviving relatives: the fact that it was addressed to both Muriel and Sylvia raises the question of whether he thought he had been forgiven yet by Sylvia, for going back to France. Perhaps he was simply overworked and distracted by the job in hand. The operation would mark the first time that he had ever taken part in a full-scale infantry attack. And he was not coming to it with the nervous enthusiasm of an innocent new officer, but with all the experience of a year at the front, and the full knowledge that the odds against infantry officers' survival were low.

On the 20th the 4th Seaforths formed up outside Metz at 10a.m., but were not needed that day, and returned to their billets at 4.30p.m. They were part of the 154th Brigade, which was the divisional reserve. On that day, however, Mackintosh was seen by a 5th Seaforths' officer, R.F.Sinclair, who had been a corporal when

Mackintosh first joined the battalion in 1915. A letter to John MacLennan from Sinclair[26] said that he had not seen Mackintosh since going back to the U.K. to be commissioned, since, by the time he returned to France in 1916, Mackintosh had been wounded. On the 20th Sinclair met Mackintosh, who was at the head of his platoon, and managed to have a short conversation with him. Poignantly, Sinclair thought that he was the last person of his own battalion to have seen him.

This is the last documented evidence of Mackintosh before he went into action on the 21st. After a long apprenticeship in the trenches, sustaining bombardment and patrolling and raiding in No Man's Land, this was Mackintosh's first major attack, in the open, and in the rain. As the 51st (Highland) Division went over Flesquières Ridge its advance was recalled by two officers of the 6th Seaforth Highlanders:[27]

> The sights which we witnessed as we lay in our new
> position brought fresh hopes. There were enthralling
> scenes – the cavalry cantering into action in perfect
> formation (not, unhappily, to be maintained for long);
> the 4th Gordon Highlanders, with pipes and drums,
> marching as a revue in column of route; the sight of a
> real live battery galloping forward and coming into
> action at our ears, and the constant covey of aeroplanes
> low-flying and intrepid. We were all out on a common
> task, and the sight of the others in their might,
> enthusiasm and strength had an inspiring effect upon
> our portion of the British Army.

The pipe bands, marching columns and cavalry, galloping artillery and aircraft blended ancient and modern warfare in an unlikely and extraordinary military panorama. Mackintosh's 4th Seaforths were in the 154th Brigade of the 51st Division, leading the attack: 'And the 154th Brigade, under that very gallant Seaforth,

---

(26) Information received from John MacLennan

(27) *The Great War, 1914-1918. 6th Seaforth Highlanders, Campaign Reminiscences*, Capt. R.T. Peel, MC and Capt. A.H. Macdonald, MC, WR. Walker and Co., Elgin, 1923, page 55

General G.K. Buchanan, now took up the tale and went on with a will.'[28]

The 4th Seaforths had left Metz at 4a.m. and had crossed the previous day's battlefield, strewn with dead men, shattered trenches and rolled up barbed wire, to arrive in the old German front line by 6.30a.m.[29] At 7.15a.m. the battalion assembled about 1000 yards west of Ribécourt, then moved off past Flesquières and followed a country road past Orival Wood to the crossroads at La Justice. The 4th Seaforths and the 9th Royal Scots were supporting the leading troops of the brigade, which were forced to a standstill by the German resistance on the Cantaing Line. There was machine-gun fire from Bourlon Wood, which overlooked the battlefield, and shelling and trench mortar fire.

The 4th Gordons and the 7th Argylls were leading the advance: the former were focussing on Cantaing village and the latter were being enfiladed from Anncux. Bewsher relates:

> . . . the 4th Gordon Highlanders having been led away
> to the right, touch had been lost between the two
> battalions. A company of the 4th Seaforth Highlanders
> was therefore ordered forward to fill the gap between
> the Gordons and the Argylls.[30]

No.4 Company of the 4th Seaforths, commanded by Captain Gray, in which Mackintosh was a platoon commander, was the company brought forward. It was soon held up by the Germans at Cantaing Mill, part of the Cantaing Line. No.1 Company sent forward Sergeant Ross with a number of men and they succeeded in driving three troublesome machine-gun parties back into Cantaing, on the right. The advance had halted and enemy planes flew over the soldiers lying in the open and, according to Haldane, 'poured machine-gun fire on them'.[31]

---

(28) Peel and Macdonald, ibid, page 55

(29) 4th Seaforths' battalion war diary. Queen's Own
Highlanders Museum, Inverness

(30) Page 252 *The History of the 51st (Highland) Division* Major
F.W.Bewsher. Blackwood, 1921

(31) Haldane, ibid, p.241

At 11.30am the 62nd Division took Anneux. Tanks arrived at noon and with their help 4th Gordons took Cantaing village by 1.30p.m. Haldane states that Cantaing Mill, from which came gunfire pinning down the 4th Seaforths 300 yards away in the open 'sheltered two field guns beside machine-guns'[32] and held out until 3.30p.m. when:

> the situation was cleared up by the arrival of seven tanks, which moved forward followed by the 7th A. & S.H. and the company of the 4th Seaforth Highlanders,[33] and that Captain Gray . . . was wounded at about 1p.m., while Lieutenant E.A.Mackintosh was killed and Lieutenant MacGregor was wounded.[34]

How, precisely, did Alan Mackintosh die? The obituary in *The Times* of Tuesday 4th December1917 could not say, though it does state that he was killed: '. . . while observing enemy movements under heavy fire.'[35]

Murray's 'Memoir' says: '. . . He fell, shot through the head.'[36] This information is likely to have been obtained by Murray from Mackintosh's family when the 'Memoir' was being prepared. It is not known if he was moving forward to obtain a clearer view of the enemy, if he raised his head to see better, if he was the target of a sniper, or the victim of random rifle or machine-gun fire from enemy trenches or aircraft. The words 'shot through the head' are specific enough to indicate that a bullet was the cause of death, but could perhaps be a euphemism for a messier shell wound, the change being made in the Commanding Officer's letter of condolence to ease the grief of Mackintosh's relatives.

It is interesting to consider whether Mackintosh's bad eyesight obliged him to expose himself to greater than usual danger in order to observe the Germans. Along with his men he would be seen on the nearby horizon by the German defenders of Cantaing Mill, or

---

(32) Haldane, ibid, p.241

(33) Bewsher, ibid, p.252

(34) Haldane, ibid, p241/2

(35) *The Times* Tuesday 4th December 1917

(36) 'Memoir' *War, The Liberator* ibid, page 4

on emerging from the sunken road that may have taken his 4th Seaforths company safely through the horizon.

Whatever the circumstances, he had, in all probability, a swifter death than he had envisaged in the poem 'Death'. Nor did he become one of the missing. He was buried in the small military cemetery at Orival Wood,[37] on the road between La Justice and Flesquières. 'C.D.' also mentioned in his obituary of Mackintosh[38] the poem 'War, the Liberator', said to be Mackintosh's last. Since it was one of a number that apparently arrived home after Mackintosh's death, it is possible that he was working on it shortly before going into action, or at least still had it with him in billets. It is addressed to the authoress of a poem, who has angered him by dealing with the subject of war from an outsider's point of view. He does not deny the horror of war in his reply, but wishes to convey a combatant's experience and feelings:

> You that never knew its joy, never felt the glow of it,
> Valour and the pride of men, soaring to the sky.

The apprehension seen in 'Peace Upon Earth'[39] about the kind of life awaiting soldiers after the war reappears in 'War, the Liberator' with some force:

> Say what life would theirs have been,
> that it should make you weep for them,
> A small grey world imprisoning the wings of their desire?

With ironic reference to early views of involvement in battle, Mackintosh begins to develop the poem into a more personal account:

> All they dreamed of childishly, bravery and fame for them,
> Charges at the cannon's mouth, enemies they slew,

---

(37) Plot 1, Row A, Grave 26 (Commonwealth War Graves Commission, Enquiries Department)

(38) *The Times* 4th December 1917

(39) *A Highland Regiment* E.A.Mackintosh, John Lane, Bodley Head, 191, page 44

Bright across the waking world their romances came for them,
Is not life a little price when our dreams come true?

If 'War, the Liberator' is Mackintosh's last poem, then the last
stanza, in all its fervour, is effectively his final statement of how he
faced the prospect of death:

All the terrors of the night, doubts and thoughts tormenting us,
Boy-minds painting quiveringly the awful face of fear,
These are gone for ever now, truth is come tormenting us,
Night with all its tricks is gone and our eyes are clear.
Now in all the time to come, memory will cover us,
Trenches that we did not lose, charges that we made,
Since a voice, when first we heard shells go shrilling over us,
Said within us, 'This is Death – and I am not afraid!'[40]

Had Mackintosh survived he would have had to face the loss of
yet another close friend, his fishing companion, Andy Fraser. After
the Cantaing Line was broken the village of Fontaine Notre Dame
fell to the 7th Argylls and the 4th Seaforths, but, during a German
counter-attack on the 22nd, Fraser was mortally wounded near his
Company H.Q.[41] By the time the battalion withdrew to Metz on the
23rd, 35 officers and men were dead, 197 were wounded and 87
missing.

Although Mackintosh had been with the 4th Seaforths when
he died, he was still fondly remembered by Captain Sutherland of
his old battalion. When Captain Sutherland compiled his *History of
the 5th Seaforths*, he chose to write at length about Mackintosh, the
only comrade featured quite so extensively:[42]

On the second day of the battle fell dear old
E.A.Mackintosh, the author of *A Highland Regiment* and
War, The Liberator, familiarly known as 'Tosh', poet,
littérateur and hail-fellow-well-met to one and all. His
happy smile and cheery personality will long be

(40) *War, The Liberator* ibid, page 13
(41) Haldane, ibid, page 247
(42) Sutherland, ibid, page 143

remembered by us, while his topical songs often cheered us on our way. Of a truly poetic temperament, he laughed away all his troubles, and helped to cheer even the most lugubrious members of the battalion by his humour and fun.

Despite the doubts and torments he experienced Mackintosh had always revelled in the company of his fellow soldiers, which must have been of positive assistance in alleviating his darker moments. Sutherland returns to the subject of the raid in the Labyrinth:

> And yet beneath it all he had a very sympathetic heart. I remember at the time of the raid for which he won the M.C., after he had helped to carry in the wounded, how he broke down and wept bitterly because after carrying one of his wounded men over 100 yards through the Bosche trenches, with the Bosche following closely behind, he had to abandon him at the enemy front line, the man dying of his wounds when they had hoisted him out of the trench.

Mackintosh never really recovered from the pain of that day, when he led into action the men who, according to Sutherland, 'loved him and would do anything for him.' They had considered him to be unkillable. As with so many other young men in the Great War, this was never likely to be the case.

In the few short years before his death, however, he established a collection of literary works which does live on, albeit sadly neglected for decades after the war. He is commemorated in his home town of Brighton, and in Oxford. In the quiet graveyard of Reay, in Caithness, his name is featured on the Sutherland family gravestone after that of Private David Sutherland, the subject of 'In Memoriam': the stone says 'See Lieutenant Mackintosh's book of poems for honours. P.40.' Thus Mackintosh is commemorated in the land of the 5th Seaforths.

The 4th Seaforth Highlanders erected a cairn topped by a wooden cross on the Cambrai battlefield, in memory of those who died. The memorial was re-erected in Dingwall, Ross-shire, in 1924 by the 4th Seaforth Reunion Club.[43] Mackintosh's name is amongst those of his comrades on the memorial panel. He is, by the exceptional circumstance of a battlefield monument being brought home, remembered in the heart of the country that was his spiritual home.

In Edinburgh, when American Scots subscribed to a war memorial in Princes Street Gardens, his philosophy from 'A Creed'[44] was chosen to go below a frieze which depicts civilians being transformed, like himself, into temporary warriors:

> If it be life that waits I shall live for ever unconquered,
> If death I shall die at last, strong in my pride and free.'
> E. ALAN MACKINTOSH 1893-1917

(43) 'Forgotten Poet of the Highland Division', John MacLennan. Article in the *Glasgow Herald*, November 1974
'Invergordon in the Great War' , Catherine Mackay, and Anne McCulloch, with Primary 7 pupils of Park School, Invergordon

(44) *A Highland Regiment* ibid, page 43

The Scottish American War Memorial, West Princes Street Gardens, Edinburgh
Mackintosh's words from the poem 'A Creed' are under the frieze

Brighton College

Lieut. Ewart Alan Mackintosh, MC

Seaforth Highlanders

Killed in action in France, November 21st, 1917

EPILOGUE
WAR, THE LIBERATOR

After his death Mackintosh's mother and sister arranged for a posthumous volume of poems, *War, The Liberator*. The contract was signed by Lilian Mackintosh on February 20th 1918. On 11 September 1918 John Lane wrote to Lilian Mackintosh:[1]

> *War the Liberator* is going fairly well, but we have hit on an idea which will help both the books in getting better known. It has been suggested to me that two of the poems – 'Miserere' and 'Christ in Flanders', from *A Highland Regiment* would make very nice little, what I might call, Christmas pamphlets or cards. I have, therefore, approached a very talented young Scotch artist, who is a beautiful engrosser and decorative artists, to write out the poems and illuminate them.

No royalty was offered for the cards, which were to cost 1/-, although twenty to thirty free copies were offered to Lilian Mackintosh. Lilian Mackintosh agreed and the publication went ahead. On 20th December 1918 she wrote to Mr Willett of John Lane's saying,[2] 'I do not like the 'Miserere'. I think it is almost impossible to illustrate these pieces and I did not think it could be satisfactory.'

The most forlorn memento of Alan Mackintosh's anthologies is a royalty account dated October 16th 1925, in which the total sales of *A Highland Regiment* numbered eight, and of *War, The Liberator* only three. The royalties were for 4/3d (less than 25p).[3] This is less a reflection of his poetry than of a world that had new

---

(1) Harry Ransom Humanities Research Center, University of Texas at Austin

(2) HRHRC, ibid

(3)HRHRC, ibid

problems to face, and that wanted to put the horrors of the war behind it.

The family kept in touch with Sylvia for some time. She is recorded as having left her full-time post as a nursing member of the VAD at Earls Colne in December 1917.[4] After the publication and press notices for *War, The Liberator* Lilian Mackintosh wrote to the publishers on 17th September 1918:[5]

> Would you send me another complete set of the cuttings
> of reviews of *War, The Liberator.* I enclose a 7/6 Postal
> Order. I hope it will still be possible to get them as Miss
> Marsh wants them very much indeed.

They were unavailable and on the 20th September she wrote:

> Please do not trouble about it at all because it will be quite
> easy for me to get our own set typed for Miss Marsh.

Sylvia overcame her grief and may have continued to practise the skills she had learned in the VAD hospital. In her marriage certificate she was described as a masseuse. On 12 October 1922, at the age of 32, she married David Christy, who was 28, a farmer from Margaretting Hall, Ingatestone, near Chelmsford. Sylvia's address on the marriage certificate was Ingram House, Stockwell Road, London. The wedding took place at the Friends Meeting House, Purley.[6]

The last words are an extract from a letter to Muriel Mackintosh from R. Tait McKenzie the sculptor of the Scottish American war memorial in Princes Street Gardens, Edinburgh:[7]

> I am using two lines from one of your brother's poems
> as the epitome of what the youth of Scotland felt at the
> outbreak of the War. He had the true poet's vision, and,
> like many another, finished his career before his time.

---

(4) British Red Cross records

(5) Harry Ransom Humanities Center

(6) Julian Duffus, research historian and genealogist

(7) Rosemary Beazley

Robert Goddard at the 4th Seaforth's Fontaine Notre Dame memorial in
Dingwall, 1977 (see Chapter 4, The Labyrinth)

John MacLennan

BIBLIOGRAPHY

Adcock, A. St.John *For Rememberance* Hodder & Stoughton, 1918

Cooper, Bryan *The Ironclads of Cambrai* Souvenir Press, 1967

Bewsher, F.W. *The History of the 51st (Highland) Division, 1914-1918.* Blackwood, 1921

Edmonds, Brig.-Gen. Sir James E. *Military Operations, France and Belgium, 1916* Volumes 1 and 2. Macmillan & Company Ltd., 1932

The English Review 1910-1914.

Farrell, Fred A. *The 51st Division War Sketches* Jack, Edinburgh, 1920

Graves, Robert *Goodbye To All That* Jonathan Cape, 1929

Guinness Rogers, J. *An autobiography* Clarke & Co, London, 1903

Haldane, Lt.Col. M. *A History of the 4th Battalion Seaforth Highlanders* Witherby, 1928

Housman, Laurence (Ed.) *War Letters of Fallen Englishman* Gollancz, 1930

Imperial War Graves Commission *The War Graves of the British Empire* Section 1496-1499. Published in 1930 (Includes the Register of Orival Wood Cemetery)

The Imperial War Museum. 'Graduating-in-arms' Souvenir booklet of No.2 O.C.B., Cambridge, December 1916-May 1917

James, Brigadier E.A., OBE, TD *British Regiments, 1914-1918* Samson Books

Lear, Edward *Gromboolian Poems* Macmillan Childrens' Books (Picturemacs), 1983

Mackintosh, Lt. E.A., MC *A Highland Regiment* John Lane, The Bodley Head, 1917

Mackintosh, Lt. E.A., M.C. *War, The Liberator* John Lane, The Bodley Head, 1918

MacLennan, J.M. 'Poet of the Seaforths' (article) *Scots Magazine* May 1974

MacLennan, J.M. 'Forgotten Poet of the Highland Division' (article) *Glasgow Herald*, November 1974

Malcolm, George *Argyllshire Highlanders 1860-1960* The Halberd Press, 1961.

McKay, C., McCulloch, A., and pupils of Park School, *Invergordon. Invergordon in the Great War*

Officers Died in the Great War 1914-1919 (Reprint) Samson, 1975

Oxford Poetry, 1912-1917 Blackwell

Peel, Capt. R.T., M.C., and Macdonald, Capt. A. H., MC *The Great War, 1914-1918* 6th

The Queen's Own Highlanders Museum, Inverness. War diaries of the 4th , 5th and 6th Battalions, the Seaforth Highlanders. (Contemporary records as opposed to the printed books by Haldane and Sutherland)

Seaforth Highlanders, Campaign Reminiscences W.R. Walker and Co., Elgin, 1923

Rorie, Colonel David., DSO, TD, MD, DPH *A Medico's Luck in the War* Milne and Hutchinson, 1929

Scott, Bain and A.D.M. *7th Battalion Argyll and Sutherland Highlanders. The Great War 1914-1919* Commemorative book. Alva, 1924/5

St.Paul's School, London. 'The Pauline'. School magazine, editions from 1910-1912, and December 1917 (obituary of Mackintosh)

Ross, Capt. Robert B. *With The Fifty-First in France* Hodder & Stoughton, 1918

Soldiers Died in the Great War 1914-1919 Part 64. Seaforth Highlanders (Ross-shire, Buffs, The Duke of Albany's). (Reprint) J.B.Hayward & Son, 1988

Sutherland, Capt D., MC. *War Diary of the 5th Seaforth Highlanders* (51st Highland Division) John Lane, 1920.

Westlake, Ray. *The Territorial Force 1914* Ray Westlake-Military Books Pub.1988.

Whalley-Kelley, Capt. W. *'Ich Dien', The South Lancashire Regiment 1914-1918*. Pub.1935

Who Was Who 1897-1916. 1951-1960. 1961-1970

Belfast Evening Telegraph 5/6/1916 and 6/6/1916 (obituaries of Ptes. McDowell and Thompson in the Labyrinth raid)

The London Gazette 1915 and 1916

The Times articles 18/5/16 (the Labyrinth raid), and 4/12/17 (obituary of Mackintosh)

GLOSSARY

ANZACS: Australian and New Zealand Army Corps

Battalion: at full establishment approximately 1,000 men, customarily down to 650 effectives or below owing to casualties, leave, etc

Bomb: see grenade

Bombers: grenade throwers

Bombing officer: tactical specialist in the use of grenades. Other specialist officers covered transport, signalling, machine-guns, sniping, and trench mortars

Boche/Bosche: German – also know as Huns, Jerries or Fritz

Brigade: composed of four infantry battalions, and supporting troops.

C.O.: Commanding Officer, in charge of battalion

Corps: composed of several divisions and supporting troops

Company: four fighting companies, a headquarters and specialist sub-units to a battalion

Commissioned officer: second lieutenant and upwards

Division: composed of three infantry brigades, a pioneer battalion, and supporting troops

Down the line: away from the trenches

Enfilade: fire at the enemy from the enemy's flank, hitting from front to the rear of his troops

Entente cordiale: agreement in 1904 formalising an end to Franco-British colonial disputes: not a military alliance, although its existence aided the British drift to war

Grenade: explosive contained in ovoid cast iron designed to fragment: made by Mills (UK). Used in siege warfare in earlier times, revived for clearing sections of trench

Kitchener's army/ division/ battalion: Lord Kitchener's appeal for volunteers drew people into the regular army, forming New Army Service battalions, beginning with K.1 – the first 100,000

Maxim: Hiram Maxim invented the machine-gun, a belt fed weapon with a high rate of fire. UK version manufactured by Vickers

Military Cross (MC): established in Dec.1914 for acts of bravery – for officers up to rank of captain and warrant officers

Military Medal: bravery criteria equivalent to those of MC – for N.C.O.s and other ranks

Mortar: a modern version of siege artillery: fired a bomb in a high arc to drop into enemy trench.

N.C.O.: non-commissioned officer, lance-corporal, corporal, sergeant, company sergeant major

New Army: see Kitchener's Army

O.C. Officer Commanding a sub-unit of a battalion

O.C.B. Officer Cadet Battalion: after the ad hoc arrangements for commissioning officers early in the war an O.C.B. structure was established to run six month courses for would-be officers

Parapet: front edge of a trench

Picket: sentry

Platoon: four platoons and a headquarters to a company

Sap: trench extended ahead of the front line in the direction of the enemy to facilitate egress to No Man's Land: could be covered

Sapper: private soldier in the Royal Engineers, title derived from historic purpose – digging saps

Salient: promontory of territory projecting into enemy lines: vulnerable to attack and gun fire from front and sides

Shrapnel: shell designed to burst above ground and shower an area with shot. By common usage also the shards and from any explosion

Smoke helmet: early gas mask

Spaeter: German grenade manufacturer

Subaltern: second lieutenant or lieutenant

Temporary rank: acting, unpaid, battlefield promotion

Territorial Forces: formed in 1908 for home defence

T.M.B. Trench Mortar Battery – a number of trench mortars operating as a unit

Officer Training Corps: established in 1908, to provide military training for potential Territorial Force officers

Up the line: into the trenches

Back Endpaper:
Cantaing Mill.
Flesquieres Ridge off bottom left, Fontaine Notre Dame off top.

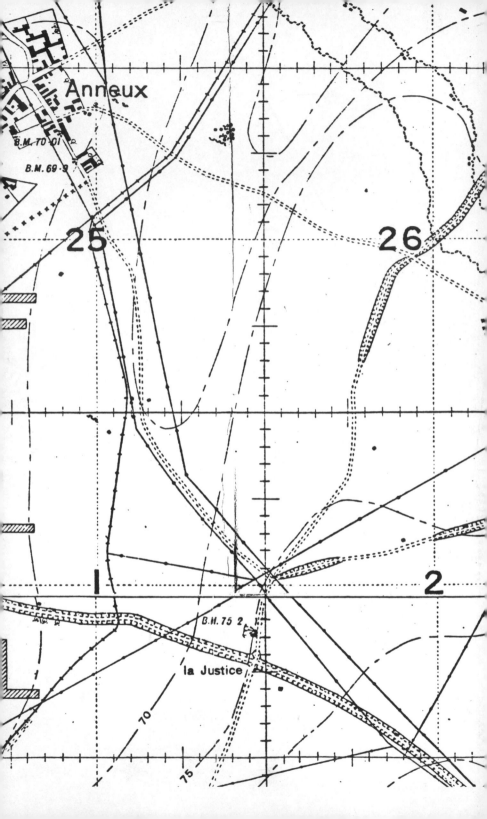